the call to
LEAD

Also by Bill Hybels

The Power of a Whisper
Holy Discontent
Just Walk Across the Room
The Volunteer Revolution
Courageous Leadership
Rediscovering Church (with Lynne Hybels)
Honest to God?
Fit to Be Tied (with Lynne Hybels)
Descending Into Greatness (with Rob Wilkins)
Becoming a Contagious Christian
(with Mark Mittelberg and Lee Strobel)

Also by John Ortberg

Love Beyond Reason
The Life You've Always Wanted
Everybody's Normal Till You Get to Know Them
If You Want to Walk on Water, You've Got to Get Out of the Boat
Living the God Life
God Is Closer Than You Think
When the Game Is Over, It All Goes Back in the Box
Faith and Doubt
The Me I Want to Be

Also by Dan B. Allender

Encouragement (with Dr. Larry Crabb)
The Wounded Heart
The Healing Path
How Children Raise Parents
Leading with a Limp
To Be Told

With Tremper Longman III

Bold Love
The Cry of the Soul
Intimate Allies
Breaking the Idols of Your Heart
Bold Purpose
The Intimate Mystery

Previously published as *The Leadership Library*

the call to

LEAD

FOLLOWING JESUS AND LIVING OUT YOUR MISSION

Bill Hybels
John Ortberg
Dan B. Allender

ZONDERVAN.com/
AUTHORTRACKER
follow your favorite authors

ZONDERVAN

The Call to Lead

When Leadership and Discipleship Collide
Copyright © 2007 by Bill Hybels

Leading Character
Copyright © 2008 by Dan B. Allender

Overcoming Your Shadow Mission
Copyright © 2008 by John Ortberg

Requests for information should be addressed to:

Zondervan, *Grand Rapids, Michigan 49530*

ISBN 978-0-310-49594-9

Cover design: Faceout Studio
Interior design: Matthew Van Zomeren

Printed in the United States of America

12 13 14 15 16 17 18 /DCI/ 21 20 19 18 17 16 15 14 13 12 11 10 9 8 7 6 5 4 3 2

Contents

Introduction

> The word of the LORD came to me, saying, "Before I
> formed you in the womb I knew you, before you were
> born I set you apart; I appointed you as a prophet to the
> nations."
>
> Then the LORD reached out his hand and touched
> my mouth and said to me, "I have put my words in your
> mouth. See, today I appoint you over nations and king-
> doms to uproot and tear down, to destroy and overthrow,
> to build and to plant."
>
> *Jeremiah 1:4–5, 9–10*

Jeremiah received a tough calling from God: to speak God's
word to God's people. The words God wanted Jeremiah to speak
were words of warning to shake them up and wake them up. But
nothing goes well for Jeremiah. No one likes what he has to say.

God tells him to keep speaking, so he does. He gets beaten and
put on display for shame. And in Jeremiah 20, he tells God how he
feels: "You sweet talked me … and I bought it. This isn't what I had
in mind." Jeremiah was torn between being faithful to his calling and
his ache for success.

The call to lead is never easy. And it often requires us to priori-
tize faithfulness over success. We must learn to give up the ache to be
successful in the eyes of the world and go with what God is calling
us to do. Leaders of God's people always sense this inherent tension
to their calling: in their ministry, in their personal life, and in the
pursuit of their God-given mission.

This collection of three essays by Bill Hybels, Dan Allender, and John Ortberg is based on talks that were given at Willow Creek Association's Global Leadership Summit. In the first, Bill Hybels discusses the challenges that leaders face when the laws of leadership don't align with the teachings of Christ. Modern business practice and scholarship have finely honed the laws of leadership, telling us that we're supposed to leverage our time, choose a strong team, and avoid unnecessary controversy. But what happens when the accepted "laws" of leadership and the demands of discipleship—the call to be faithful to Christ—collide? Using stories from his own life and ministry, Bill Hybels shows how the laws of leadership sometimes crash headlong into the demands of discipleship, and how the decisions leaders make at that point will affect the destiny of those they lead.

In the second essay, Dan Allender suggests that we lead best by revealing our true character to those we lead. Though everyone agrees that character plays a critical role in leadership, we are also aware of the fact that the best leaders are not perfect people. Instead of hiding their weaknesses, good leaders learn to recognize them and allow them to be transformed into strengths. After all, how can we be renewed and restored without acknowledging the reality that we are marred? Paradoxically, it is in our brokenness that we have our greatest opportunity to reveal the heart of God's goodness, and the greatest opportunity to strengthen our leadership.

In the third and final essay, John Ortberg talks about the importance of knowing and following the mission that God has given to us. A mission is the highest purpose to which God calls us, but every mission always has a "shadow" mission—an unworthy substitute. If they are ever to overcome their shadow mission, leaders must learn to identify and name it. From the story of a young Hebrew girl named Esther come the lessons that allow leaders to not only defeat their shadow mission, but to fully live out the authentic mission to which God has called them.

Leadership is critical to church vitality, and good leadership depends on the level of commitment, the authenticity of character, and the clarity of mission that a leader possesses. Though following God's call to lead is never easy, it is always worth the cost. Learn to wrestle with the tension and to answer the call to become the leader God has called you to be. The future of the church rests in the hands of leaders who are willing to faithfully answer that call.

CHAPTER ONE

When Leadership and Discipleship Collide

Bill Hybels

Hands down, the single most impressive leader in the history of the world is Jesus of Nazareth. Now, I don't say that just because I'm a card-carrying Christian, which I am, but because I believe the facts speak for themselves. No leader ever cast a more expansive or breathtaking vision—nothing less than the redemption of the planet— than did Jesus Christ. No leader ever built a higher-impact team in a shorter period of time with less talent to work with. No leader ever instilled deeper values or inspired people more than Jesus Christ—in many cases, enough for them to die for the cause. Certainly, no leader has ever changed the course of human history the way Jesus did ... and is still doing, more than two thousand years later.

I'd say it all adds up to some pretty compelling leadership evidence: He was the best leader ever.

BREAKING LEADERSHIP LAWS

Imagine my surprise recently when I decided to read through the New Testament book of Mark and noticed several occasions when Jesus seems willfully to violate well-known, widely accepted laws of leadership. My observations were more than a little shocking.

Imagine my surprise recently when I decided to read through the New Testament book of Mark and noticed several occasions when Jesus seems willfully to violate well-known, widely accepted laws of leadership.

Build a Team of Highly Qualified Leaders

The first place I noticed the greatest leader in human history breaking a fundamental law of leadership is in the very first chapter of Mark. Jesus has just lost his strongest ally, John the Baptist, who has been thrown in prison for taking the leaders of the day to task on their sinful behavior. John may have had some odd culinary preferences and rather minimalist taste in attire, but you can't ask for a better ministry partner. He is bold, fearless, and fully devoted to the cause. Losing John to a jail cell is a huge hit to Jesus, and the pressing question on his mind must be, *Who in the world do I recruit to replace a superstar like John?*

Jesus is a religion teacher, so how about adding a rabbi to the ranks? Or a highly trained Pharisee, maybe, or a well-respected Sadducee? What about some brilliant students of the Torah, a few leader types who are well schooled in Jewish custom?

No, Jesus goes out and instead gathers a rather motley crew of commercial fishermen. The majority of them are untrained, uncouth, and underage. Some have hot tempers, others have questionable business practices, and not one has evangelistic experience.

It is a leadership violation to beat all leadership violations, but despite everyone's raised eyebrows, Jesus plows ahead, confident he has made the right decision.

Keep Up the Momentum

The next place I noticed Jesus breaking a law of leadership is found later in the first chapter of Mark. Jesus' popularity is building. The crowds are getting larger everywhere he goes. People see Jesus driving out evil spirits, healing sick people, preaching the kingdom of

God, and they wonder if he might actually be the long-awaited Messiah. Right in the middle of this "Nielsen-rating" upswing, Mark 1:35 records that Jesus actually *withdraws* from all the action; he goes off alone to a solitary place to reflect and spend some quality time in prayer.

Obviously, this is in clear violation of the well-known law of momentum. Every leader knows how hard it is to establish momentum. And every leader knows that once you get it established, you should do whatever it takes to keep it going. Momentum is one of a leader's closest allies. When the energy's high and the team is strong and people are buzzing, the last thing you want to do is pull the momentum plug.

But Jesus walks away from it all, a decision that really miffs his disciples, who are still flying high on the buzz of effective ministry. They quickly pull together a search party and, upon finding their fearless leader, reprimand him for leaving, "Jesus, everyone is looking for you!" Which is simply code for: "What's up with this? We've all been busting our backsides to get this kingdom dream realized for you, and now that we're on a roll, you want time off for a spiritual retreat?!"

From a leadership perspective, Jesus' seclusion makes zero sense, and the disciples know it. The greatest leader of all time violates a Leadership 101–level law, to the great shock of his followers ... and me.

Propagate Good Press

Soon afterward, a man with leprosy approaches Jesus and says, in Mark 1:40, "If you are willing, you can make me clean." A hush settles over the watching crowd. Ants stop. Birds stare. Angels lean forward from their seats in heaven. Everyone knows that this diseased man has lived a pitiable existence his entire life. Leprosy has left him disfigured, excluded, and, according to Jewish custom, ceremonially unclean. The one person on the planet who possesses the power and authority to take away his physical, mental, and emotional anguish, Jesus Christ, now stands just two feet from him. Talk about a media event in the making!

Jesus knows the guy is in a sorry state. He also knows that the man is about to be completely and instantaneously healed. Facing a pending miracle of this magnitude, any leader worth his salary and bonuses would summon his PR folks and sanction a full-scale press conference. Rally the reporters and get the cameras rolling! This one will blow viewers away!

A hush settles over the watching crowd. Ants stop. Birds stare. Angels lean forward from their seats in heaven.

Mark 1:41 says, "Jesus ... reached out his hand and touched the man." As a result, the man's leprosy departs from his body. But instead of trumpeting his success on the evening news, he looks at the leprosy-free man and says, in verse 44, "See that you don't tell this to anyone."

Surely it was just a lapse in leadership judgment on Jesus' part. I mean, if you're trying to magnetize people to your mission, the last thing you want to do is *squelch* good press!

Avoid Unnecessary Controversy

Every leader knows that it's impossible to please all the people all the time; it's one of those leadership truths that just comes with the territory. But seasoned leaders also understand that stirring up *unnecessary* controversy should be avoided at all costs. In other words, if you're going to receive some kicking and screaming as a result of a hard decision, then at least be sure it's the right decision, made at the right time. Why spend credibility capital if you don't have to?

A pastor called me a while back. He was from a very conservative church that was right in the middle of its largest capital campaign ever. One of the elders wanted to open up a discussion about changing the anti-alcohol policy that the church had upheld proudly for a hundred years. The pastor was inclined to agree with this elder and asked for my opinion on the matter. I answered him in two words: "Not now!"

Then to clarify, I said, "Take my word for it: you must be *very* careful not to stir up unnecessary conflict during critical eras of church building. Open up that issue for discussion at some point, maybe, but *don't* do it now."

When I read the second chapter of the Gospel of Mark, however, I found an instance where Jesus completely disregards this law of avoiding unnecessary controversy.

By way of context, Jesus has just completed several miraculous healings, including the now-famous one where a paralytic man is lowered through a hole in the roof into a meeting room where Jesus is speaking. The man wants to be healed, and nothing is going to stop him from landing in the presence of the One who can heal him.

As a result of all this fanfare, the crowds surrounding Jesus and his followers are building once more, and townspeople are all brimming with energy about Jesus' miraculous ministry. Momentum is on Jesus' side again, and everything seems to be heading up and to the right.

Until one day — a Sabbath, mind you — when Jesus decides to get some fresh air with his disciples. They wind up walking through some guy's grain field, and the disciples start popping the heads off several stalks to snack on. The Pharisees, who never seem to be far from the action, absolutely go nuts and consider the grain-popping motion an act of labor, which is strictly forbidden by their rules. If Jesus allows this sort of reaping on the Sabbath, they think, who *knows* what's next?

Jesus explains the whole bit about the Sabbath being created for people, not the other way around, but the Pharisees aren't easily dissuaded. They turn on their heels and head off to set their

It was not the brightest of leadership decisions, you might say . . . at least on the surface. All things considered, would twenty-four hours really have made that big a difference?

next trap for Jesus. Before long, they will lure him into committing yet another Sabbath infraction and as a result have him turned over to the Herodians, the group which will ultimately plot his horrific death.

Talk about having stirred up a hornet's nest of controversy! Really now, couldn't he have waited until *Monday* to take the disciples on their little joy walk?

It was not the brightest of leadership decisions, you might say … at least on the surface. All things considered, would twenty-four hours really have made *that* big a difference?

Leverage Time and Influence

As if all of the preceding violations aren't enough, Jesus makes another colossal leadership blunder in Mark 10, when he breaks the law of wisely leveraging time and influence. Every leader knows that you only have so many hours in a day; to be effective, you must figure out which people will move the mission ahead the most and then spend time with those people. The rest of the folks are going to have to find their own way. You have a job to do, and to do it well, you have to leverage your influence with the people who can make things happen. Again, this is one of those no-brainer fundamentals of leadership.

In verse 13, Jesus is caught spending time in the middle of a workday with a group of children. Surely there are more important things he can be doing: preparing sermons, leadership development, strategic planning, whatever. Blowing his afternoon on a bunch of pesky half-pints makes no leadership sense. The disciples are all too aware of this, so they decide to take matters into their own hands. They tell the kids, as well as the parents of the kids, to get lost: Don't they know that Jesus has very important things to do, people to see, places to go?

Jesus is a little less than thrilled by the disciples' interference. He severely rebukes them for pushing the children away and, in essence, says, "I alone will decide who is worth my time and energy, whether you guys agree with me or not. If I want to hang out with kids, it's my prerogative, no matter what leadership law gets violated."

Don't Bite the Hand that Feeds You

How about another one? Shortly after that occasion, Jesus thoroughly alienates a very wealthy man. Remember his interaction with the rich young man? This breaks a cardinal rule pertaining to fundraising: Don't make wealthy people mad! You'll probably need their help sooner or later, so don't offend them without good reason. But Jesus goes right for this rich man's jugular, spiritually speaking. And sure enough, Mark 10:22

Jesus thoroughly alienates a very wealthy man. . . . This breaks a cardinal rule pertaining to fundraising: Don't make wealthy people mad!

reveals that this first-century investment-banker-type heads off, having made *no* contribution to Jesus' cause. You tell me: was that wise leadership on Jesus' part?

Still want more?

Avoid Sensational Exploits

In Mark 11, Jesus cleanses the temple of money changers and marketers who are peddling their wares in a house of worship. (It actually *needed* a good cleansing, but that's beside the point.) Jesus' motivation may be pure, but any student of leadership has to wonder if the whip (John 2:15) is really all that necessary. All the whip is going to do is give the press something to sensationalize, and seasoned leaders never give free bullets to the opposition. If he has to turn over a few tables, fine, the point has to be made. But lose the whip. Where's the common sense there?

Demonstrate Unshakeable Courage

Perhaps the most extreme example of Jesus breaking a leadership law occurs just before his betrayal and arrest in the Garden of Gethsemane.

In Mark 14 we find the city of Jerusalem in an uproar. There are vicious rumors floating around that someone will be paid to kill Jesus and his disciples. The emotional climate is intense.

So, to counterbalance the fear his followers are feeling, what does a veteran leader like Jesus Christ do? One might think he would demonstrate unshakeable courage and then call his followers up to his level of steadfastness, à la William Wallace in the movie *Braveheart*. When his soldiers were thinking about defecting from an impending major battle, Wallace (played masterfully by Mel Gibson) mounts his horse and rides back and forth in front of all the soldiers, shouting, "I am not afraid to die for our cause on this day, and you shouldn't be either!"

Being wobbly and weepy when the stakes are high ... is that really the best way to serve the team and the cause?

Talk about inspiring! After seeing that scene, even I was ready to sign up for action. Which is huge, given the fact that I am a notorious chicken when it comes to fighting and hate violence of any kind.

With fear-stricken disciples huddled around him in the Garden of Gethsemane, Mark 14:34 reveals an extremely distressed, deeply troubled Jesus: "My soul is overwhelmed with sorrow," he admits, even "to the point of death." Jesus asks three of his men to join him in prayer—a heartfelt prayer in which he asks his heavenly Father if the mission that was assigned to him could please be amended or taken away. To paraphrase, he says, "Take this cup from me if at all possible, Father. But, if not, then your will be done."

It's a far cry from *Braveheart*.

And a far cry from any sort of adherence to the leadership laws I know. The laws I know dictate that leaders must never show personal vulnerability in the midst of a mission-threatening crisis. Being wobbly and weepy when the stakes are high ... is that really the best way to serve the team and the cause?

Now, to be clear, despite Jesus' moment of fear, he quickly finds the courage to get up, endure horrendous suffering, and voluntarily lay down his life for sin-scarred people like you and me. He does precisely what he has come to earth to do. He completes his redemptive mission. But that momentary transparency into his emotional struggle — the display of weakness and uncertainty in the Garden — makes me wonder what this leader was thinking!

LEADERSHIP VIOLATIONS COMMITTED BY YOURS TRULY

I read through the entire book of Mark, noting these very interesting situations where Jesus seems to violate long-held laws of leadership, and, to be perfectly honest, it was a bit unsettling. I began to wonder: *Have I ever, throughout the course of my thirty-plus years in leadership, knowingly broken the laws of leadership?*

> *I began to wonder:* Have I ever, throughout the course of my thirty-plus years in leadership, knowingly broken the laws of leadership?

To my surprise, nearly half a dozen violations came to mind.

Bet on a Ragtag Team

The very first law I broke was when I decided who would be on the church-planting team that would establish Willow Creek Community Church. Every leader knows how important it is to surround yourself with the highest caliber people you can find: the brightest, most capable, most competent ones available. But for some strange reason, I took a completely different course of action when God prompted me to start Willow. Instead of recruiting high-capacity types, I surrounded myself with a few personal friends, none of whom had any specific experience, expertise, or talent in church work.

One friend was fresh out of the military and trying very hard to get off a bad marijuana habit. Another was just back from South

America, where his missionary parents had dragged him along. To say he was spiritually disillusioned would be a gross understatement: he didn't have much use for God, he didn't go to church, and he was intolerant of anything that smacked of religiosity. Another was a high school buddy who had dropped out of college because he had no clue what he wanted to do with his life.

These guys were no *Who's Who* in church planting.

The leader in me knew that I was signing up for all sorts of unnecessary risk with this ragtag group, but whenever I prayed about who was supposed to help me start Willow, the Spirit would whisper the same three names over and over again: *Tim, Scott, and Joel.* So that's who I chose. Thirty-one years later, these guys are still with me; it can accurately be said that Willow Creek Community Church was built on their shoulders as much as mine.

Of course, I would never advise a young church planter or a business entrepreneur to assume this measure of senseless risk when launching a brand-new endeavor; I'd never suggest putting such fragile eggs in the basket of an inexperienced ad hoc group of non-leaders. But that's exactly what I did. I knew I was headed down a path that seemed to violate a critical leadership law, but I also knew that God was the one leading. And so I followed.

Derail the Momentum Train

When I read the occasion in the first chapter of Mark where Jesus seemingly disregards the law of momentum, a memory from my own leadership journey sprang to mind. In the late eighties, Willow was growing by hundreds of people a month, and reporters began to write articles about "this ministry in Chicago" that was rapidly becoming the largest church in North America. Despite the positive attention, I had the sickening feeling that even though people were filling up our auditorium, they weren't necessarily becoming fully devoted followers of Christ. This was a problem for one simple reason: our mission was (and still is, actually) to turn irreligious people into fully devoted followers of Christ.

We were building a crowd, but we weren't building committed followers. We weren't facilitating the type of growth that would one day birth an "Acts 2 church"—a people marked by their acceptance of seekers, their devotion to Scripture and prayer, their generosity with material possessions, their consistency of fellowship, and so forth.

I spent some time with God hashing through this dilemma. I rallied some of my most trusted friends and advisers and, after factoring in their assessments and advice, I made my toughest ministry decision to date: I intentionally derailed our momentum. I interrupted whatever was on the preaching docket to do a six-week series about the cost of following Christ, including no-holds-barred teaching about the requirements of discipleship. I wanted our entire congregation to understand what "full commitment to Jesus Christ"

> *I made my toughest ministry decision to date: I intentionally derailed our momentum.*

really meant. It was during this time that I coined the expression: "Ninety-five percent commitment to Christ is 5 percent short."

I asked every person in the auditorium why on earth they would consider giving less than their *absolute* best to the One who had given his best for them. I beat that drum for six weeks straight.

This approach certainly flattened out our growth curve. Worse than that reality, though, was the nagging realization that I'd developed a split personality. The leadership side of me screamed, *You're an idiot! You wrecked the church's momentum!* while another voice whispered, *Way to go, Bill! You're doing exactly what I want you to do. You're not just building a crowd; you're building fully devoted followers of Jesus Christ. You're really trying to establish an Acts 2 church here, which is exactly what I called you to do. Way to go!*

The law of leadership fought tooth and nail to maintain momentum. But the quiet voice of the Holy Spirit told me something entirely different. This wouldn't be the last time the dichotomy occurred.

Embrace Muslims after 9/11

I have a fairly high risk tolerance, so there are numerous examples of my stirring up unnecessary controversy. In this regard, I relate to Jesus' lawbreaking tendencies quite well. One instance in particular came to mind as I sat with pen in hand after my read-through of the Gospel of Mark. It had to do with a decision I made on the heels of 9/11.

Three or four months into our nation's healing following the terrorist attacks, things were still quite difficult for Muslims. In Chicago, for example, people were beaten on the street just because they were adherents of Islam; mosques were firebombed; death threats were made ... all because of the backlash of 9/11. It was a senseless, heartless response to an already dreadful situation, and I felt that our church should do its part to put an end to the insanity.

I invited a local Muslim leader to attend our weekend services as a resource for greater understanding. I wanted to do a fifteen-minute interview about the true teachings of Islam and felt whatever risk I assumed was well worth it if it meant helping Willow's congregation grasp what the Koran really teaches about infidels, jihads, holy wars, violence, revenge, and other oft-misunderstood issues.

The goal, I kept reminding myself, was to build bridges by fostering acceptance and expanding perspectives. But that's not how things went down.

A conservative Christian magazine caught wind of the interview and proceeded to distort the facts in what can only be characterized as a nationwide, months-long *creaming*.

Interestingly, most people at Willow thought the service was extremely beneficial, that it did indeed serve as a bridge builder in our community. But I had risked a fair amount of national credibility capital and created "unnecessary controversy" on that one.

Spend Time with Sam

Jesus seemingly violated the law of wisely leveraging time and influence when he blew an entire afternoon on a posse of kids. This is another law-breaking experience I can relate to.

Years ago, Willow engaged in an arduous effort to address an eighteen-million-dollar shortfall in our capital campaign. Other senior leaders and I were in the middle of conducting dozens of "vision tours," where I would lead hard-hat-clad Creekers through the parts of the new facility that were under construction and cast vision for the ministry that would take place there, once everything was funded. In addition, I wrote letters inviting people to give their best gifts — time, talents, treasures — to this effort. I met one-on-one with scores of donors and asked if they would pray about how they might help us.

Every moment of every day mattered — a lot! — during that era. But one afternoon, I did something that would have sounded the alarm bells in even the most novice leaders.

I answered my ringing cell phone to discover a man named Sam on the other end. Sam lives in South Haven, Michigan, where my family spends part of our summers. My wife, Lynne, and I had helped Sam buy a car wash one year so that he could keep his family from falling into a state of total financial ruin. Over a crackly connection that afternoon, Sam said he needed my help.

It took me two and a half hours to drive from Willow's campus in South Barrington to the car wash in South Haven, which is a long time to question the wisdom of taking such a trip. I arrived, greeted Sam, and took my seat across from him on an overturned five-gallon bucket in one of the wash bays. Pretty casual accommodations for a staff meeting, I thought, but I had bigger concerns on my mind, like, for starters, what on earth am I doing here when Willow obviously is destined for disaster?

Sam proceeded to tell me that he was a hundred and eighty dollars short that month. Personally, he didn't know how he was going to pay the rent and the electric bill, not to mention feed his family.

He began to describe his regrettable state of affairs to me, but I found myself struggling to pay attention. My mind was spinning a little regret-fueled tale of its own: *I can't believe you wound up here.*

You're some kind of leader, Bill, dropping everything, getting into your car, and lugging yourself all the way to Michigan, believing that somehow, someway, your random act of kindness would make a difference. Look at you, sitting here on a bucket, messing with Sam's hundred-and-eighty-dollar problem, when you should be leveraging your time with people who can help with the EIGHTEEN-MILLION-DOLLAR predicament you're in back home!

That day, sitting with Sam on those overturned buckets in the car wash, I felt a *collision* of sorts, different from anything I'd ever known in my life. The leadership side of me was saying: *Get back to Barrington, Bozo! This is no time for charity; this is no time for sentimentality; this is no time for your heart to bleed for the condition of the poor. You can solve that when the campaign is over, but for now, get your rear in gear and get home!*

At the same time, another voice whispered: *I am so proud of you, Bill. Hang in there with Sam; dollar figures aside, his problem is just as big to him as yours is to you. I'm in this; I'll help you both meet the demands you face. For now, just be a friend to Sam.*

Jesus' words from Matthew 25:40 tipped the scales toward the voice vying for discipleship: "Whatever you did for one of the least of these brothers and sisters of mine, you did for me." As I drove away from the car wash that day, I sensed the whisper of the Spirit saying, *Bill, I'm working on you. Trust me, please. I'm working on you. Sam doesn't need your help as much as you think he does; rather, you need what happens when you relate with him.*

I stayed the course with Sam until we could sort out his financial woes, and I will remember that meeting in the wash bay for a long, long time.

I wonder, do you know what that intersection collision between leadership and discipleship feels like? Have you established ahead of time which you will choose when the collision occurs? I remember well the first time I had to take my own medicine on this issue. It happened on a beautiful June morning, at a fishing derby, of all places.

Prioritize the Fishing Derby

Special Friends is a ministry to more than fifty Willow families that have children with serious mental or physical challenges. Over the years, I have established some extraordinary friendships with some of these very brave young kids and their parents, but there's nothing necessarily rational about the soft spot in my heart I have for them; as those who know me well can attest, the spiritual gift of mercy is noticeably absent in me. Still, whenever I can sneak into one of the Special Friends activities, I do.

One summer, our Special Friends ministry was holding its annual fishing derby at the lake on our campus and sent me a personalized invitation to attend. I gladly put it on my schedule, but then some travel complications made me doubt whether it would all work out. As the Saturday morning of the derby drew near, things weren't looking good. I tried to rationalize my way out of feeling guilty for missing the event. I listed five airtight reasons why a leader with my level of responsibility had no business having a fishing derby on his calendar and why such an event should be an easy one for me to miss with no qualms whatsoever.

Interestingly, though, the Spirit of God wasn't buying my excuses. He hounded me, chased me down, and just wouldn't let go. I'm not prone to hearing audibly from God, but honestly, it felt like the Spirit was saying to me in full voice: *Bill, if you get this decision wrong, if you can't fit this event into your carefully crafted, highly leveraged leadership schedule, you've lost the plot entirely. If you bow out of this event, I'm here to tell you, you are* seriously *screwed up!*

It began to feel like my presence with the Special Friends that day was a kind of pass/fail test for my inner person. I would soon learn that it was the focal point of a much deeper lesson God was trying to drill into me. I finally stopped rationalizing, justifying, and struggling about the whole deal; I changed a bunch of other plans and declared, once and for all, that I was going to the fishing derby.

I had a ball! I helped kids put worms on their hooks and toss their lines out into the lake, and I celebrated with each and every one of them as they caught fish. I did my very best to add to their joy and enthusiasm that bright, sunny day, but when I drove home from the campus after the event had come to a close, the Spirit sort of killed my sunshine: *It shouldn't have been that hard, Bill. It really shouldn't have required this much of a struggle to get you to show up.*

Questions from heaven started popping up like little thought balloons above my sunburned head: *What's happening to you, Bill? Why was that such a traumatic decision? You better slow down your pace. You better think this stuff through, because plenty of these kinds of decisions will come your way in the future. Maybe now would be a good time to sort out how you will respond. Maybe you need to figure out what happens when the laws of leadership and the demands of discipleship collide, because every once in a while, they will. Mark my words.*

Interestingly, though, the Spirit of God wasn't buying my excuses. He hounded me, chased me down, and just wouldn't let go.

Although the Spirit had given me a great book title, I was none too thrilled about the content: I knew I had a *ton* of work to do before I could provide answers to the issues he raised in my heart and mind on the trip home from the derby. I decided to commit every spare moment of discretionary thought time to this question: What will be my response when the laws of leadership and the demands of discipleship collide?

In the weeks and months to follow, I searched my soul, studied the Scriptures, talked to friends, and reviewed my leadership journey. Even now, I do not have it all figured out. But perhaps a few of my initial reflections will trigger thoughts and observations and opinions of your own as they pertain to this all-important question for every leader to answer.

THE ORIGIN OF THE "LAWS OF LEADERSHIP"

The first task I undertook was to clarify what these "laws of leadership" really were and to ascertain where they originally came from.

Author and leadership expert John Maxwell is a close personal friend, but when a guy like that puts out a book titled *The 21 Irrefutable Laws of Leadership*, and it sells millions of copies and helps leaders in every discipline around the world, doesn't it make you scratch your head a little? For me, some pretty interesting questions started surfacing. Like, are there really just twenty-one leadership laws? What if there are nineteen? Or twenty-eight? What if there are *two hundred and eighty-three* laws of leadership? Who chose twenty-one, anyway? And who gets to decide how these laws get described?

> *Here's what I'm beginning to grasp: laws of leadership are really just descriptions of hard-learned lessons that, for hundreds of years, leaders have come to view as valuable guides toward mission achievement.*

Here's what I'm beginning to grasp: laws of leadership are really just descriptions of hard-learned lessons that, for hundreds of years, leaders have come to view as valuable guides toward mission achievement. Laws of leadership are, in essence, a collection of wisdom principles, passed from one leadership generation to the next. The principles can pertain to building profitable companies or championship athletic teams or fantastic, God-honoring ministries. They can be learned on the battlefield or in the boardroom, during training camp or a political campaign. The "laws" that emerge serve as boundary lines, in a sense, that denote the field of play. Step outside of them and leadership's penalty flags are likely to start flying.

That said, leadership laws are not "inspired" by God in the same manner that we use the word *inspiration* when referring to Scripture. They are not inerrant, infallible, or immutable in the way we understand those terms biblically, but they are *extremely* valuable

> *Leadership laws are not "inspired" by God in the same manner that we use the word* inspiration *when referring to Scripture. They are not inerrant, infallible, or immutable . . . but they are* extremely *valuable observations.*

observations that, when followed, can cause each successive generation of leaders to get better at leading whatever they're leading.

WHEN LEADERSHIP AND DISCIPLESHIP DOVETAIL

After nailing down my beliefs about the origin of leadership's laws, the first conclusion I came to regarding how to respond when discipleship demands intersect with those laws was this: I believe that, most of the time, the laws of leadership and the teachings of Scripture — particularly regarding embracing people living far from God and discipling those who have already made a faith decision — dovetail nicely. I think that collisions between leadership and discipleship are actually quite uncommon.

Jesus consistently manifested what we might consider traditional "leadership laws" throughout his ministry: he cast and consistently reinforced a God-given, crystal-clear vision. He was perpetually (annoyingly, even!) "on purpose"; he poured into his team until the mission poured out of them; he resolved conflict immediately . . . with love *and* truth; the list could go on and on.

The violations — or apparent violations — that I referenced from the Gospel of Mark caught my attention because they were rare exceptions to Jesus' strong, steady, mostly predictable leadership patterns.

It has been my strong bias for the last thirty-plus years that Christian leaders must take full advantage of the accumulated teachings of every leadership generation that has gone before them. What we work for in ministry leadership is the single most important endeavor on planet Earth — the building of the kingdom of God. The potential of this kingdom is greater than any other, and the stakes involved in realizing it are higher. When we get it right, and especially when we don't, we impact people's *eternities*. It seems plain to me, then, that Christian leaders above all others would strive to be the most devoted, most faithful, most *astute* learners of leadership's laws.

In my opinion, good teaching will never be enough to build the kingdom of God. But combine good teaching with great leadership, and watch what God will do! I believe that theology and the laws of leadership can synergize

> *It seems plain to me, then, that Christian leaders above all others would strive to be the most devoted, most faithful, most astute learners of leadership's laws.*

beautifully, catalyzing growth at exponential rates in churches, ministries, and businesses. It's for this reason that I continue to challenge leaders: Read everything you can read about the laws of leadership. Go wherever leadership is taught. Get near leaders who are more advanced than you are. Keep growing. Keep challenging yourself! Keep getting better!

But there is more.

Shortly after the realization that leadership and discipleship rarely collide, a second conviction emerged as a result of my focused attention on the issue.

DECIDE ON THE SIDE OF DISCIPLESHIP

In those rare cases when the human laws of leadership and the scriptural demands of discipleship *do* collide, decide on the side of discipleship every time. *Decide on the side of discipleship every* single *time.* Trust the promptings of the Holy Spirit, for they will help you at these deadly intersections.

Much of the published leadership literature these days has come from secular leaders in secular arenas. While we can learn a lot from people in business and athletics and government and the military and so on, we cannot forget that, ultimately, Christians—in whatever arena they lead—are trying to build *God's* kingdom. From time to time, leadership lessons from the secular world do not translate well into the arena of kingdom building, and, as ministry leaders, we must remember that our operating values and our ultimate marching orders come from only one book—a book that is God breathed, Spirit inspired, perfect in its content, unchanging in its ability to transform lives.

When the demands of discipleship articulated in the Bible collide with human laws of leadership, read my lips: Defer to the Bible. Look to the Bible. Trust the Bible. And obey the Bible … *every* time.

Several years ago, I was asked to conduct an interview with an exceptionally bright, very capable young man who was being considered for a role on our staff. I was alerted by my colleagues, who had already met with this candidate, that he should pass the interview with flying colors. "He's fantastic! And we really need him," they explained. "Only ten minutes of your time is necessary for this one, Bill. Really, it's only a formality … we just need your final sign-off."

But five minutes into the interview, I felt trouble brewing in my spirit. I could see how smart and capable this person was, but I also saw a few red flags. In my opinion, he had an air of overconfidence that bordered on being prideful. I didn't want the interview to get ugly, but the Holy Spirit kept whispering: *Probe this, Bill. Push on it and see how he responds.*

So I pushed. And once again, his response was very alarming to me.

Despite this young man's obvious competence and talent, he was not at all open to my queries about pride. He refused to have a candid conversation about how he would behave in a structure of authority. He shut down when I tried to investigate his views on the differences between having independent strength versus contributing to the strength of a team. And from there, the interview became very difficult.

Now, the leadership laws would say: Look, he's a young buck with some rough edges, but the guy's potential is huge. Those rough edges will be ground off while he's making great gains for the organization, so just hire him.

The teachings of Scripture, however, are quite clear on pride and its implications. First Peter 5:5 says, "God opposes the proud but shows favor to the humble." Proverbs 16:18 notes, "Pride goes before destruction, a haughty spirit before a fall."

These verses and others flooded my mind. The whispers of the Spirit seemed to be shouting in my ear: *Take a pass on this guy. Leave the position open. Pray with the young man, wish him well, but don't you dare hire him.* No matter what the leader in me said to do, I knew I had to let this guy go elsewhere.

> *When the demands of discipleship articulated in the Bible collide with human laws of leadership, read my lips: Defer to the Bible.*

The candidate had terrific leadership potential, and I'm sure he could have catalyzed some very exciting activity around Willow Creek. But I couldn't disobey the Spirit by hiring him. At that interview, my understanding of Scripture collided with the laws of leadership, and I simply had to land on the side of discipleship. I slept well that night. I knew I had done the right thing.

Even in secular arenas, there will be times when you need to follow the demands of discipleship rather than the laws of leadership. Just because you lead in a secular context does not mean that you, as a believer, don't have the Spirit whispering wisdom into your mind and heart. At those times, friend, *listen.* And obey.

The interview experience I describe above has occurred numerous times for a COO of a large public company in the Midwest. A Christ-follower, he can't always explain to his nonbelieving CEO and board members why certain candidates who are stellar on paper don't pass muster with him. But after repeatedly ignoring the Spirit's whispers and suffering the consequences, he now views *every* key interview as a spiritual act of worship. "Guide me, God," he says quietly as he enters these situations. In his opinion, the Holy Spirit's enablement is the only way he can preserve his personal values, protect the integrity of his staff culture, and execute his leadership role with credibility. I wholeheartedly agree.

I know of a property manager in Michigan, a believer who had nearly half a million dollars extorted from him last year. The culprit was his personal finance associate, also a professing Christ-follower. Talk about a dicey situation: the property manager's attorney (not to mention his justice-seeking wife) advised him to consider a hefty lawsuit, but something in him wouldn't allow it. "I kept getting the feeling God was up to something bigger than restoring my bank account," he said.

This much I know: you can't put a price tag on being obedient to the Holy Spirit's promptings. Even when you are the only person who understands why you are doing what you're doing, walk confidently along the path God paves for you.

He followed through on those promptings from the Spirit. In a move that stunned everyone involved, he refused legal action and committed himself to restoring the decades-long friendship with his former finance associate. He continues to trust God's promise of provision to cover daily living expenses—expenses that never used to enter his mind.

Sounds crazy, right? This much I know: you can't put a price tag on being obedient to the Holy Spirit's promptings. Even when you are the only person who understands why you are doing what you're doing, walk confidently along the path God paves for you.

Fellow leader, I'm challenging you to be a Christ-follower who really does seek God's kingdom first. Be Jesus' disciple in whatever arena you lead and conform yourself to his image in whatever situation you find yourself. Keep Christ first whenever the laws of leadership and the demands of discipleship collide.

THE MINISTRY OF THE HOLY SPIRIT

Perhaps by now you're thinking: *But how do I know? I mean, when it gets right down to one of those collisions, how do I know what to do?*

The best response I can offer is simply a reminder that the ministry of the Holy Spirit is a very real, very accessible gift to be opened by every Christ-follower. John 16:13 promises that the Holy Spirit *always* will guide us down the best path, if only we will listen to his promptings. The Holy Spirit will give us God's mind on every matter when those collisions look inevitable. The longer I lead, the more dependent I become on his ministry and his whisper, not just for what I do at collision points but also — and especially — for day-by-day encouragement, guidance, and wisdom in all aspects of my life and my leadership.

It takes more than human-crafted leadership laws to be effective; the role of Scripture and of the ministry of the Holy Spirit can never be overestimated.

Christian leaders cannot afford to wield influence apart from the direction of the Holy Spirit. It takes more than human-crafted leadership laws to be effective; the role of Scripture and of the ministry of the Holy Spirit can never be overestimated.

As I consider afresh how true it is that we as ministry leaders cannot operate apart from the Holy Spirit's work in our lives, I can't help but remember a time I probably would have imploded if it hadn't been for the Holy Spirit's intervention.

During a tough ministry season, the general responsibilities of my role and some challenging extenuating circumstances were ganging up on me. Criticism was mounting, and I was in a pressure cooker to beat all pressure cookers. I knew if I didn't get away and spend some private time with God, I was going to blow. It wouldn't be a pretty sight.

I drove away from the Willow Creek campus, got on a boat, and took it out on Lake Michigan, as far as I could from any sight of land.

You should know that I don't make a habit of asking for signs and wonders from God, but on this particular day, that's exactly what I did. I needed a word, a signal, *some* indication from God that the seemingly devastating leadership complexities I faced wouldn't take me out of the game altogether. "God, please let me hear from you. I know I'm supposed to be more mature than this, but today, I'm not. I need some kind of reassurance here that I'm not in this alone. I can't keep leading the charge if I feel like I'm all alone."

I know this may sound mystical or maybe a little silly ... or even presumptuous. But on my knees on the deck of a boat in the middle of a lake, it's precisely what I said to God.

And in response to my agonized request, there was silence. Perfect silence.

For a while, I wondered if God was otherwise occupied, but before my faith could falter, God gave me three thoughts. He conveyed them so forcefully and with such clarity that I ran below deck, grabbed a pencil and paper, and began to scribble them down so that I could remember them exactly as they were given.

Here was thought number one: *Bill, you are a treasured child of the most high God.*

> I sat and I read those words over and over again that day on that boat. And I cried. I'm a treasured child of the most high God. How could I have lost sight of that?

That was the phrase, exactly as I received it: "You are a treasured child of the most high God." Every word in that phrase was a gift to me. Bill, *you*, with all your faults and sin and junk and with all the fear you have right now; *you are*—you are right now, not someday when you get to heaven, someday when you're stronger and you have your act together better than you do today; you are right now a *treasured child*—not an orphaned child, not a stepchild, not even a mildly appreciated child. You are a treasured child of the *most high God, the most high God,* through whom all things are possible.

It was like God was saying: *Bill, remember who you are. And remember whose you are.*

I sat and I read those words over and over again that day on that boat. And I cried. *I'm a treasured child of the most high God.* How could I have lost sight of that?

The second thought that came to me from the Spirit went like this: *The cause that I have assigned to you is going to prevail, and the combined forces of darkness cannot defeat it.*

> When you have face-to-face issues, problems, or confrontations with others, it's all different when you've first been face-to-face with God.

What a powerful reminder! Somewhere along the way, I had forgotten the words of Jesus, who said, in essence, in Matthew 16:18, "I'm going to build my church, and the gates of hell won't prevail against it."

That revelation lifted a heavy, heavy burden off my shoulders. I thought: *Yes, I'm involved in a really tough battle right here, right now; but the church of Jesus Christ has survived two thousand years of battles, many of which raged a whole lot hotter than this one. God is going to make sure that his church survives and thrives until Christ's return. The ultimate responsibility for the victory of his church is on his shoulders, not mine.*

Then came the Spirit's final words that day: *I have surrounded you with some of the most loving, remarkable Christ-followers in the world. Lean into them. Let them love you. Invite them into your struggle. Ask for their help. Ask for their prayers.*

Within hours of getting back to the dock, I did just that.

The great leader T. D. Jakes once told me that when you have face-to-face issues, problems, or confrontations with others, it's all different when you've first been face-to-face with God. Although my experience on the boat that day may seem crazy, it enabled me to get face-to-face with God. And that made all the difference. My circumstances had not changed one bit, but by the time I got back to the dock that afternoon, my spirit had shifted, my heart had expanded, and my courage had regained its footing.

My point? Just a simple reminder that the power of the Holy Spirit is the leader's best friend. The one who stands alongside you when leadership gets lonely ... that's the Holy Spirit. The one who guides and gives you strength when leadership gets confusing ... that's the Holy Spirit. The one who warns you of pitfalls and whispers words of renewal when you grow weary ... that's the Holy Spirit. The one who reminds you that you are a treasured child of the most high God ... *that's* the Holy Spirit.

If you know the laws of leadership and follow them when they should be followed, if you love God and readily follow the prompting of his Spirit when you sense he is guiding, then you will make it.

Maybe the Holy Spirit wants to remind you right now, in your role as a leader, that the cause God has assigned to you is indeed going to prevail. God's kingdom will be built. His name will be glorified. But it's not all on your shoulders. Christ has secured the victory.

Or maybe you are going through a high-stakes challenge and you've never opened up your heart to the people around you to tell them how hard your challenge is. Friend, if God has surrounded you with remarkable, loving people, then lean into them. Try facing the challenge as a team instead of alone, as an individual. Maybe you need to show the kind of vulnerability Jesus showed in the Garden of Gethsemane when he said, essentially, "You know what? This is hard. It's *really* hard."

If you know the laws of leadership and follow them when they should be followed, if you love God and readily follow the prompting of his Spirit when you sense he is guiding, then you will make it. And when there's a collision, if you say, "I'm going to decide on the side of discipleship and the clear teachings of Scripture every time. I'm going to put my hand in the Holy Spirit's hand all day, every day, and allow him to be my guide and my strength," then you will make it.

In fact, you won't just "make it"—you will thrive. You won't just thrive—you will *prevail*! And you will be able to overcome whatever the forces of darkness throw at you, guaranteed.

FIGHTING WORDS

The proof of that guarantee is in one little verse, found in the book of Nehemiah.

Nehemiah and the people had been working day and night to rebuild the broken-down wall around Jerusalem, and right in the middle of their backbreaking efforts, enemies sent word that they were going to come in with troops and massacre the whole lot of them.

Understandably, the people were more than a little jittery.

Knowing he had to make some sort of leadership move, Nehemiah gathered everyone together and gave them a challenge. In essence, Nehemiah 4:14 says, "Remember God, who is great and awesome, and then fight with all your might."

I love those words! *Remember God*—he is for you. He loves you. He is more than just enough. You are a treasured child of the most high God. And then, *fight with all your might*—give the cause of Christ your all!

As you face your daily responsibilities as a leader, this is my simple charge from Nehemiah straight to you: Remember God, who is great and awesome. Remember God, who is faithful and true. Remember God, who is ever-present in times of turmoil. Remember God, who has promised to pull you through.

And then the second part: Fight with all your might. Fight for the lives and hearts of people far from God. Fight to recruit volunteers. Fight for resources for the poor and the forgotten. Fight to build a business that serves with integrity and distinction. Fight to save God's creation and to bring peace and justice to earth. Fight to build schools and communities and organizations that reflect God's kingdom. Fight *with all your might* for your church to become a full-blown Acts 2 expression in your community.

Whatever your leadership endeavor, give God all of the glory. And one day we'll all meet in heaven, where we can celebrate his goodness forever.

CHAPTER TWO

Leading
Character

Dan B. Allender

How did you first become a leader? Do you remember the circumstances? Maybe you earned an actual title to indicate you were the person in charge—the captain of the team, a candidate for public office, the CEO. Perhaps other people gravitated toward you naturally, counting on you for decisions and willingly following your lead. Or it's even possible that your leap into leadership resembled mine—and came about more or less as a matter of default.

I was teaching at Mars Hill Graduate School, which was, at that time, a satellite school of Western Seminary in Portland, Oregon. We were, however, in the process of moving the school toward independence, and six of us who were on the faculty were involved in this transition. At one point, about three years into the process, we were required to complete and sign an accreditation document. And one of the blanks on that form required an answer to this question: Who is the president?

I'll never forget that meeting. When it got to the point where someone had to consent to list their name as the president, the room got very quiet. As we looked around at one another, it became clear no one was going to speak. We were all testing each other, waiting to see who would be foolish enough to agree to such a thing.

Eventually, we reached a consensus that because I was the oldest, I would take on that position—although no one, including me, expected that I would ever really act as the president.

That assumption continued until the moment when, about four months later, we faced our first dismissal of an employee. And with that responsibility, I may have become the only human being in history ever to fire the same person three times in less than twenty-four hours.

We are to have a character that invites others to see the goodness of Christ and to be a character that intrigues and compels others to discover what it means to be forgiven and set free to live with passion and joy.

I fired him, providing due cause and asking him to think and pray about our conversation. At the end of our forty-five minutes of interaction, I said we would speak again the next day, never imagining he would go home and create an entire plan as to how he could enhance his performance and revise his job description. He came back eager for the opportunity to present his plan—and it was clear the firing had not taken effect.

I gathered enough wisdom and strength to fire him again. At that juncture, he asked, because of certain things he was doing, if he could stay another week to ten days to finish those projects. I considered that an enormously gracious suggestion on his part. "How reasonable," I thought. So he went back to work.

Later that day, our receptionist—who had previously worked for a large corporation—asked me, "Is he still employed?" "Yes," I said, "but just for another week to ten days."

At that point, she began to enumerate all the things this person had access to and explained how this could be very problematic if he harbored any kind of ill spirit toward the school. Well, I hadn't even thought of an ill spirit, much less the complications that could occur. She told me that in her previous job, when employees were asked to leave, the company allowed them an hour or so to go to their desks and gather all of their personal belongings. Then they were escorted out of the building.

It made sense! Which meant I had to fire him for the third time.

And that was only the beginning. In the years that followed, I made every classic mistake a leader can possibly make. Then I invented some I don't believe ever before existed on the face of the earth.

But every mistake became a lesson learned. And very often these hard-earned lessons prompted valuable conversations with other leaders. I began to see that certain patterns surround outstanding leadership. I noted, for example, how often the leaders I most admired are each widely known for their strong, highly regarded character. That is not to say that they are stodgy, unimaginative, play-it-by-the-book kinds of people. In fact, most are quite honest about their struggles in ministry and with the wars of leadership.

Yes, they have impeccable integrity, but they also make me laugh. They not only wow me with their individuality and spontaneity, they impress me with their meticulous honesty and forthrightness. They struggle and worry about their kids. While they are committed to their marriages, at times they feel lonely and need more support from their spouses. They are real, human, fully alive, and beautiful people.

Too often, leaders suppress such openness. What they are allowed to say from the platform or in conversations with others is narrowed down to the "expected and tolerated," and all else must be hidden or denied. Such limitations create a degree of being two-faced—one face public, the other private.

At times that hypocrisy is even internalized. When this happens—when we deny the parts of ourselves that would cause disruption if they were seen or acknowledged in polite company—we are on shaky ground. Because no one can live long with such disparity without a loss of integrity.

No one is immune to the public-private face war. Sometimes the face we present in public requires immense courage; other times, the public face is an indication of great cowardice. Are you aware of when you have been courageous or cowardly? I pray that by reading and then reflecting on this material you will be encouraged to consider both possibilities.

Eventually, I came to realize that leadership is all about character. And that the Christian leader, no matter what he or she oversees, has the opportunity to be a *leading character*—an example, a living representation of the power of the resurrection and the privilege of the fellowship created by sharing in Christ's suffering.

We demonstrate what it means to be a "leading character" by living this reality before those who are part of our organizations. We communicate our vision and strategies, we support and affirm our employees, we strengthen successful programs, we scrap processes that are no longer effective, and far, far more. But never should we do these things without making Christ known through word and deed. The primary focus is not what we speak, but how we live. We are to *have* a character that invites others to see the goodness of Christ and to *be* a character that intrigues and compels others to discover what it means to be forgiven and set free to live with passion and joy.

In short, the most effective leaders invariably embrace two fundamentals in this regard:

- The first is to *have* a character.
- The second is to *be* a character.

HAVE A CHARACTER

Say the word *character* and a dozen associations come to mind. There are character witnesses and character actors. We live in a culture all too familiar with character assassination. And we're intuitively aware of whether the behavior displayed by someone we know is "in character" or "out of character."

Primarily, though, we associate the presence of character with virtues, including honesty, courage, and truthfulness. Few compliments are more valued than to be regarded as a person of outstanding character. Everyone would agree that a leader's character is a key component of a leader's effectiveness.

Our character reflects our creator. We are made in the image of God, and the nature of God's personhood is woven into the deepest fabric of our being. To understand our character, we must begin with a glimpse of God's character.

God's Character

Since every human being—the believer and the unbeliever—is made in God's image, we all bear a character that *reveals* God. What does it mean for us to reveal God in our personhood, through our personality, and through our character? One of the most concise ways to sum up this very nature of God is found in Psalm 62: "One thing God has spoken, two things I have heard: that you, O God, are strong, and that you, O Lord, are loving" (vv. 11–12 NIV 1984). In a few words, the psalmist captures the essence of God's character—*strong* and *loving.*

God's strength is absolute and is in no way dependent on anyone or anything outside of the Godhead. God is fully God, lacking nothing. God is also love, and he has chosen to bind himself with loyal covenantal passion to his creatures. God is free and bound, independent and utterly committed.

How can both of these be true? Many would argue that if God is strong, he can't also be loving—since so much suffering exists in the world and he has done nothing, apparently, to end it. Such logic further suggests that if God is loving, then he can't be strong, since God's love would then be predicated on his power. But the conundrum is ours, not God's. God is both strong and loving, and this presents no contradiction or conflict for the Trinity.

God's strength is reflected in his sovereign authority over all that exists and all that transpires. Nothing happens that is a surprise or out of his control. He has authority because he is the author. And while he is not the author of sin, he uses even that to accomplish his sovereign purposes. Look at God's boast to Job:

> Who shut up the sea behind doors
>> when it burst forth from the womb,
>>> when I made the clouds its garment
>> and wrapped it in thick darkness,
>>> when I fixed limits for it
>> and set its doors and bars in place,
>>> when I said, "This far you may come and no farther;
>> here is where your proud waves halt"?
>
> *—Job 38:8–11*

God's creative power and ordering of the world is part of his strength. His strength is also demonstrated by the boundaries he set for how we are to live, and both his law and the consequences for transgression reside under his authority. The fullness of his power, however, cannot be cataloged and understood; it can only be honored with awe and obeyed with reverence.

Yet, God is more than power; God is love. Scripture is filled with comparisons and descriptions meant to help us grasp the depth and inclusiveness of God's holy and never-ending love for us. That love is compared to the tender compassion of a mother for her child, for instance, and God is portrayed as bending his knee to whisper kindness to encourage his child's faint heart. We are told God's love seeks us even in the angst of longing and hurt, and we are frequently reminded of his mercy and loving protection. As is the case with his power, the fullness of God's love cannot be cataloged and understood; it can only be honored with gratitude and offered to others in reverence.

God uses his strength and love for honorable and wise purposes. He is fiercely loving and tender to his people. And we have been made to reflect God's character in all of our relationships.

Our Character

The actual word in the Greek—*charaktér*—originally was used in connection with tools designed for engraving. And character is indeed a tool that marks us—that in one sense cuts us, shapes us, and engraves us. We are image-bearers who are intended by God to make him known in a fashion that no one else on the earth can do in the same way.

Our marking is as unique as a snowflake. From a distance we all look reasonably alike, yet upon closer scrutiny our engraving is phenomenally distinct. Each person is engraved with a marking—face, body, parents, intellect, birth order, talents, passion, burden, and calling—that is different from any other human being. Our character is a complex interaction between God's writing of our body and background, the contributions others make to our life, and our unique participation in cowriting our story with God. The totality is our character, how our "marking" appears to others.

In Greek philosophy, character became a list of virtues that were considered requisite of a good citizen. You can see how the word then came to mean our reputation and, eventually, how it began to represent a series of virtues that one must desire and work to attain. If one lacked these virtues, then one had a bad character; if one succeeded, then one possessed a good character.

As simple as this seems, it must be underscored that the gospel compels us to live out a paradox: The more progress we make, the more we need grace. The more righteous we become, in fact, the more we are aware of how deeply we are flawed and how much we need forgiveness. Character development—described as a simple increase in virtue—is not, therefore, a Christian concept.

To better understand our character and how it affects the organizations we lead, we must see how God has marked us, how sin has marred us, and how God has chosen to remake us in the image of Christ.

We Are Marked

The nature of our character is our marking—and because we are made in God's image, every one of us has the marking of God's glory.

So how are we to use those attributes of God's glory? What are we instructed to do as a result of being made like God?

The two attributes that reveal the glory of God—that show the marking, or character, of God in our lives—are the same two the psalmist uses to describe God's character (Psalm 62:11–12). We reveal the very character of God—in our lives and in our leadership—when we are strong and when we are loving. Being made in God's image, God has given us the capacity to move with strength and to do so with a tender heart.

> *We reveal the very character of God — in our lives and in our leadership — when we are strong and when we are loving.*

Soon after God names our identity in Genesis 1:26, he also establishes our calling, providing us with opportunities to demonstrate these God-given attributes. "Then God blessed them and said, 'Be fruitful and multiply. Fill the earth and govern it. Reign over the fish in the sea, the birds in the sky, and all the animals that scurry along the ground'" (Genesis 1:28 NLT).

This passage is often referred to as the "cultural mandate," the belief that we are to apply God's principles to all aspects of society. It implies that all people—male and female, at all times and in all cultures—are called to the same standards as a result of being God's image-bearers. It would be far too simplistic to say that we are called to make babies and farm, although these are both valid examples of our mandate.

To give birth and cultivate growth require immense strength and tenderness. We quickly learn that to be true as we live out the first aspect of the cultural mandate by launching a new business, planting a church, developing a medical breakthrough, or taking any idea through the slow process from gestation to birth. Strength and tenderness are crucial as we "tend the garden," whether we're streamlining a process, training employees, negotiating with integrity, or discipling new believers. (You can see why the Great Commission is widely regarded as Jesus' version of the cultural mandate.)

If one neglects any aspect of God's character, then neither birthing nor growing will go as God intended. Sadly, many leaders are gifted with great strength but choose to ignore tenderness. Too often, leaders are unwilling to be tender because it appears to lessen their authority or control over others. Other leaders are far more tender than strong and carefully avoid conflict with their colleagues or senior leaders. We all tend to champion one element of God's character and to excuse ourselves for ignoring or denying the other.

Let me offer an example: A friend whose daughter was diagnosed with leukemia didn't want to burden his company's employees with his personal suffering. He was deeply respected as an efficient and fair boss, but was seen as somewhat aloof and distant. As he dealt with his daughter's illness, his work became chaotic. No one had a clue as to what was going on — except for the fact he was changing before their eyes.

Learning of his problems at work, I asked him what troubled him about sharing his story with the employees. He said, "I don't want them to pity me or be watching over my shoulder." I told him that instead of pity, he was creating confusion, and even though he did not want to be watched over, that's exactly what was taking place as suspicions grew. We forget that people always watch leaders to gauge the security of their world.

Subsequently, my friend opened his heart in a company-wide meeting. He admitted that he had failed to be as tender to their daily struggles as he was now asking them to be on his behalf. The response of his company was sincere sorrow, relief, and even greater commitment. His strength had created great respect, but his absence of tenderness had created a more distant workplace. Once he allowed this tragedy to open his heart, the culture of his company improved.

Some leaders are great at providing creative vision to begin a work but are miserable at growing and maintaining movement in an organization. Others are phenomenal at supporting growth but terrified at starting something new. Seldom is this a matter of right or wrong; more often it reflects the differences in our calling and giftedness. Yet, when starters lack tenderness and maintainers lack strength, it is far more than a matter of giftedness and calling. It is a flight from growing more in the character of God.

Take a deep breath and, with pen and paper in hand, answer two questions:

- Do people at work see me as more tender than strong, or more strong than tender?
- What are the obstacles or risks involved in change?

Your strengths in one or the other are to be admired. Do you thank God for those strengths? The area of your weakness is not merely to be changed; first, it must be pondered, reflected on, and opened before God for his input.

We are men and women who are *marked* to be both strong and tender. The complexity arises because we are also *marred* by sin (see Genesis 3).

We Are Marred

Sin distorts. It dulls and diminishes the vivid marks of God's image in our lives. It negatively impacts how the character of God is revealed through our strength and tenderness. When sin does its work, these qualities of strength and tenderness become so deeply bent and marred that we fail to reveal the markings we were intended to show. And when we are marred by sin, we fail to reveal the glory of God.

The consequences of our sin become a process of hiding and blaming, just as our original parents, Adam and Eve, did after they rebelled against God. Notice that Adam and Eve hid rather than gather the strength to cry out for mercy and tenderness. Instead of having the courage—the strength—to be exposed and to bear the consequences, Adam first blamed God for having created Eve and then blamed Eve for having given him the fruit. We too fail to humbly stand before God to seek his tender mercy; we too turn against God with revolting strength to pour contempt on him—and anyone else in our line of fire—when we are exposed.

Notice that the apostle Paul expresses strong concern regarding contempt for God's kindness. He asks, "Or do you show contempt for the riches of his kindness, forbearance and patience, not realizing that God's kindness is intended to lead you to repentance?" (Romans 2:4).

Each one of us might want to stop here, for a moment, and thoughtfully answer Paul's question. Do I show contempt for the power of God's kindness? Have I forgotten that it is his tender love that draws my heart to repentance? Contempt belittles and mocks and allows us to turn away from something that unnerves us. Instead of demonstrating true strength, we too often resort to contempt. Rather than being tender and vulnerable, we flee and hide. These not only mar our character, they diminish the way we lead our organizations.

My dear friend and copresident at Mars Hill Graduate School, Ron Carucci, came into my office one day. He wasn't happy and, as he sat down, he said, "You have created a mess and I have spent the last several hours mopping it up."

I must preface the rest of the story by saying I do not question Ron's love and respect for me, but when he spoke, I immediately turned both sick and hard. I had no idea what I had done wrong and I hated to hear what was coming. Although the details are now fuzzy, my failure had been to begin micromanaging an event that already had been in process for several weeks.

As I listened to the details of my failure, I immediately began to justify in my mind what I had done. I had actually been immensely patient in a process that seemed poorly managed, I told myself, and had simply offered a few suggestions as to how it could be improved. In fact, I had been too busy (cowardly flight) to get involved, and my remarks (barely hidden contempt) were heard by those planning the event as undermining their authority.

Ron's intervention was strong and kind. I began fluctuating between skewering myself with contempt and blaming others for my failure. In a matter of mere seconds, my response was to quit—to withdraw and lick my wounds. But Ron also named that tendency of mine. He understands that if one starts surgery, it is wise not only to complete the surgery but to extract as soon as possible all the issues of flight and fight.

A leader's failure is never isolated, involving only the leader. Usually the failure of a leader involves basic patterns of hiding and blaming throughout the whole organization, patterns that must be uprooted.

We talked and prayed. It became clear to me that I not only needed to apologize and address the discouragement I had caused but, going forward, I needed to find ways to get involved early in the projects that most affected me, rather than waiting until the superstructure had been built before trying to revise it.

How obvious! Well, it's obvious now, but at the time, no one had ever before addressed this issue with me. Instead, they had hidden while viewing me with contempt for this pattern of mine. A leader's failure is never isolated, involving only the leader. Usually the failure of a leader involves basic patterns of hiding and blaming throughout the whole organization, patterns that must be uprooted. But the solution must always begin with the senior leader. If the fix doesn't begin with the leader, then any efforts to address it in the so-called rank and file will be futile.

As a consequence of our being marred, when we risk the possibility of our weaknesses or faulty motives being exposed, we grab our fig leaves and run for the bushes. And when we are exposed, because the One who knows us seeks us out ("Where are you?" God called to Adam), our natural response is to blame someone else for our actions.

Perhaps one of the most revealing, severest, and cruelest remarks ever said to God was spoken by Adam in this accusatory phrase: "The woman you put here with me—she gave me some fruit from the tree." And then, almost in a whisper as an afterthought, he adds, "Okay. And I ate it." Is that ownership? Absolutely not. It's blaming. It is a way of saying, "I'll take responsibility only if another is at fault first." We all can benefit by learning from Adam's (poor) example.

We need to seek the help of others to fully see and understand this problem of honesty and confession. I admit I am tragically blind. Without the eyes of those who see my refusal to take ownership for my failures, I will often name only a small portion of the cancer. It is often our most virulent critics and enemies who most want us to see our blindness—and who are only too willing to poke us in the eye to help us see better. Instead, go to a trusted friend, compatriot, or spouse who will tell you the truth with kindness and even tears. Ask them. Invite them. Persuade them to talk with you about your refusal to take responsibility for some ongoing failure in your life and your tendency to spread the blame to others. We are persons with both integrity and deceit. We must use our integrity to invite others to expose our deceit, our hiding and blaming.

We Are Remade

We are marked to reveal God's strength—and yet, because of sin, that strength often turns to harshness. We are marked to be tender—and yet, because of sin, we are often weak and willing to compromise. The glory of the gospel is that in spite of our failures, God has *remade* us in the image of Christ to offer a different kind of strength and tenderness. Paul says that we are new creations, new persons in Christ:

> Either way, Christ's love controls us. Since we believe that Christ died for all, we also believe that we have all died to our old life. He died for everyone so that those who

receive his new life will no longer live for themselves. Instead, they will live for Christ, who died and was raised for them. So we have stopped evaluating others from a human point of view. At one time we thought of Christ merely from a human point of view. How differently we know him now! This means that anyone who belongs to Christ has become a new person. The old life is gone; a new life has begun! And all of this is a gift from God, who brought us back to himself through Christ. And God has given us this task of reconciling people to him. For God was in Christ, reconciling the world to himself, no longer counting people's sins against them. And he gave us this wonderful message of reconciliation. So we are Christ's ambassadors; God is making his appeal through us. We speak for Christ when we plead, "Come back to God!"

—*2 Corinthians 5:14–20 NLT*

My old life—your old life—died in Christ's death. And a new heart has been birthed in us. We are being remade.

This new heart can grow to God's fullness of character. This new heart gives me new eyes to look at every human being, including myself, from the perspective of heaven; my viewpoint is no longer limited to life under the sun. This new life gives me the capacity to call all people, including myself, to be reconciled with Christ— through my appeal, through my life itself. And we need God's help to do that.

Paul gives us an extraordinary picture of the transformation of our identities as leaders who are marked, who are marred, and who are being remade:

I thank Christ Jesus our Lord, who has given me strength, that he considered me trustworthy, appointing me to his service. Even though I was once a blasphemer and a persecutor and a violent man, I was shown mercy

because I acted in ignorance and unbelief. The grace of
our Lord was poured out on me abundantly, along with
the faith and love that are in Christ Jesus.

—1 Timothy 1:12–14

Then Paul pauses, asking for our attention by saying: "Here is
a trustworthy saying that deserves full acceptance" (as if everything
else he said wasn't!). What he's trying to tell us here is, "Everything
I've said to this point is very important, but now listen very, very
carefully to this part": "Christ
Jesus came into the world to save
sinners — of whom I am the
worst" (1 Timothy 1:15).

As leaders, what are we to be
when we stand before our congregations or our organizations? I
believe one of our central callings
is to stand before the community

> *I believe one of our central callings
> is to stand before the community
> of God and the world and to say,
> in effect, as Paul did, "I am the
> worst of all sinners."*

of God and the world and to say, in effect, as Paul did, "I am the
worst of all sinners." Or we could honor Paul's prior claim to that
title by saying, "I am the worst of all sinners, except one." (Unless,
after I've told you more of my story, you would prefer to revise that
to "except two." That way, you could claim to be the third worst
sinner on the face of the earth.)

Paul claims there's not another human being — past, present, or
future — who will ever live with more enmity toward God than he
had. And part of the glory of the gospel is that this man, our apostle,
the one who in many ways brought us the fullness of Scripture, is
referring to himself when he says, earlier in this passage, that the
"law is made not for the righteous but for lawbreakers and rebels, the
ungodly and sinful, the unholy and irreligious" (1 Timothy 1:9).

Paul goes on to name the unrighteous. They're perverts, they're
liars, they're thieves, they're perjurers. He even includes these

descriptions—mother-killers and father-killers—not found in any of his other lists of grave sins.

After going through the list of abhorrent and wicked sins, he then describes himself: "I, your apostle, am the chief of all sinners; I am the worst of all." He is immensely strong in acknowledging his sin—he does not flee from the truth. He does not blame others or even himself. He is amazingly tender in confessing the wonder of being forgiven, and he acknowledges his profound need for Christ. Paul gives us a rare picture of a redeemed man who, in his role as the apostle to the Gentiles, is unafraid to make himself known to those he leads.

Extreme Makeovers

What would it mean for you to follow Paul's example and reveal your true character as you stand before those you lead? Most of us grew up believing that if we were to tell the truth, if people knew what was in our hearts ... what had just passed through our minds ... what we had been either leaning toward or falling into ... those we lead would decide we have no right to be in charge.

> *What would it mean for you to follow Paul's example and reveal your true character as you stand before those you lead?*

We know more is required of us if we are to follow Paul as he follows Jesus. And that means a profound makeover of our character and our leadership. But before we get to that, we need to understand that our culture has already undergone an extreme makeover of its own.

Our Culture

Many, if not most, of today's leaders came into their positions in a world that was deeply influenced by *modernism*. Basically, that approach to life told us that there are linear answers—principles through which, if we simply apply step one, step two, step three, step four—one after the other—our problems can be solved. We will enjoy a leadership structure that works, we will achieve relief from depression, we will have a better marriage, and we will have thinner thighs in thirty days. As a result, we have become linear, principle-oriented, and simplistically driven, wanting answers to our problems so much more than we want the person of Jesus Christ.

We see this in literature on leadership and at conferences on leadership that offer their instruction in four, seven, or twelve steps. Here are four steps to resolve conflict in the workplace, seven steps to become your organization's most effective leader, twelve steps to develop strategies for growth of your organization. The difficulty is that although the material offered may be excellent and worthwhile, the "sales pitch" is based on the implied promise that results are only four or seven or twelve steps away—and those steps can be readily tackled and performed effectively. This is also true for advice of a more personal nature. Marriage series, for instance, have been marketed with descriptions like, "In one CD you will find more hope and change than from any other single hour in your life." That is overstatement. It is pandering. It is snake oil. If there was any time in our history most likely to endure such schlock, it was during the era of modernism. But, Toto, we're not in Kansas anymore.

The dilemma for anyone still steeped in a modernist mind-set is that our world has changed. We now live in a *postmodern* world that does not accept and will never embrace some of the core assumptions of the modernist promise that mere facts and linear progress are life-changing. As a result, many people today—especially younger people—don't trust us or our leadership.

Let me, once again, tap into the wisdom of my dear friend Ron Carucci, who wrote in his book *Leadership Divide* that many fear we are facing a dearth of leaders. In fact, Ron says there are many individuals who are dying to lead but refuse to lead in the manner they have witnessed as the norm. They balk at the job-takes-all-toadvance mentality of the modernist leaders they see and are far more committed to family and friends than the modernists. They view hierarchy as a bastion of privilege, not as a necessity for making decisions. In countless ways, emerging leaders are asking hard questions — and finding the answers from their elders sorely inadequate and not convincing.

This new postmodern world is profoundly fragmented; and with that fragmentation, severely insecure; and with that insecurity, very suspicious of leaders.

This new postmodern world is profoundly fragmented; and with that fragmentation, severely insecure; and with that insecurity, very suspicious of leaders. People are so suspicious, in fact, that they're angry at virtually anything we as leaders say. Everything we say is eventually examined to gauge how sincere, how honest, and how true we really are in our positions of leadership.

Consequently, if we continue to live in a world where all we offer are step-by-step solutions — whether they be for conflicts among coworkers, or organizational failures, or marriage problems — we will never connect to the real issues with the wisdom that results when we apply strength and tenderness.

What moved us beyond modernism into this postmodern era? The world we live in now knows there are no easy answers — no easy explanations for a Hiroshima, for a World Trade Center, for a Virginia Tech. We recently ended a century that had more holocausts and more people butchered than at any other time in human history. Not surprisingly, the general consensus is that easy answers don't work. We need to step up to our responsibility as passionately committed leaders to find answers to the complex problems we face by engaging in more complex thinking.

If we respond to the problems brought to us by those we lead — whether those questions are simple or global — by slapping them with a simplistic answer using the usual linear approach of two or three principles, we will have failed. We will have planted the seeds of disappointment that can grow into both suspicion and despair and a lack of trust in our leadership abilities. Maybe the person leaves with a gracious "Thank you, that was very helpful." But I promise you, too often they leave thinking that what we offered was trite and self-righteous and didn't solve the problem.

Changing our approach, however, can pose difficulties. I spoke to one pastor, after teaching on this topic at his church, who said, "I don't differ with much of what you've said, but if I talked like you do about your struggles with God, your family, and your work, I'd be looking for work the following week." After hearing a few of his stories, I agreed with him—his job would be finished. His church was led by a group of angry, defensive, aggressive men who would not tolerate any "psychobabble" or newfangled ideas—nothing, in fact, that would not have been preached in the same way that their fathers had heard it in the same church decades ago.

For this pastor, and maybe for you as well, there is real wisdom in going slow and introducing small steps of change when examining our failures as leaders and our struggles with God. Patience is often a calling that must be embraced over many decades of ministry, even though the Bible is utterly, almost embarrassingly, honest about the shortcomings of our leaders. Consider Abraham, Isaac and Jacob, Moses and David. All these individuals were flawed, and yet the Bible doesn't flinch in telling a portion of the real story of each of these leaders. If you're a pastor, perhaps just preaching from these passages honestly and well, without mentioning any part of your own story, might be a good place to begin. Even that, however, may be more than some congregations can bear. Such was the case with this pastor, a reality that

> *We need to step up to our responsibility as passionately committed leaders to find answers to the complex problems we face by engaging in more complex thinking.*

prompted me to ask, "Are you so committed to staying that you refuse to engage in a personal extreme makeover?"

How do we bridge the gap between the two very different worlds that exist in our jobs and in our churches? How do we come to understand the thinking of the new leaders who are emerging in this postmodern world? We listen. We listen to the differences in worldview expressed. We listen without giving advice or disagreeing with their opinions. For only through listening with honest curiosity, without critiquing, can we begin to understand.

Our Character

As Christian leaders, we must see ourselves as having "leading character" that invites others to see the goodness of Christ in us. We must develop a way of thinking about leadership that allows us to be strong, yet tender, and stand before our congregations and our organizations and say that, as president or manager or pastor, our primary task is to "live the gospel before you." We must fully acknowledge that our gifts and talents are from God and reflect God's glory and beauty.

It's all about character.

In addition, we must acknowledge our propensity to sin, perhaps with an admission like mine: "I'm a marred human being—one who is full of hiding and blaming." To go deeper into our faults, look to Jesus, who expands our understanding of sin by using the words *lust* and *anger* (Matthew 5:21–30). He knows that we all struggle with these dark reactions. Lust is any desire that has gone mad and become a demand. Though the word *lust* is most often associated with sexual desire, other desires—lust for power, money, recognition—can be equally consuming. And when our desire is thwarted, we direct our anger at anyone who stands in our way, anyone who prevents us from getting what we demand—that which we believe will satisfy our need. Jesus does not take these destructive reactions lightly; in fact, he goes on to say that anyone who lusts is an adulterer and the person who is angry is subject to the same punishment as a murderer (Matthew 5:21–22, 27–28).

Jesus' words seem to be hyperbole. I may struggle with lust, but I've never had an affair. I may be angry at times, but is that as bad as killing someone? The radical makeover of our character that must take place begins when we embrace the wonder of being forgiven — but to accept forgiveness, we must first admit our need for it. So it's important for me to be clear: It isn't that I used to be lustful and angry; I am lustful and angry today and need God's forgiveness.

You may recall that decades ago, when Jimmy Carter was running for the presidency, he was asked by a *Playboy* magazine interviewer if he felt he was better than other Americans because he was a Christian. He said, "No," and added that he had struggled with lust like any other person. The reporter made his confession the featured element of the story. Jimmy Carter was held up to ridicule and made out to be a fool. Within a month his approval rating dropped by 10 percentage points. But was he a fool? If he was, then he was a fool in the same way Paul commends that we all be fools for Christ (1 Corinthians 1:18–31).

For many reasons, President Jimmy Carter is a hero. He had the courage to tell the truth, weather the consequences, and lead in a manner that has been recognized again and again as a model of peacemaking strength and fierce tenderness. His example encourages us to ask ourselves: Will I be honest, with wisdom and propriety, wiser than a serpent and innocent as a dove? And will I be tender, with honor and discretion, like a birthing mother and a compassionate father?

What is true of me, I believe, is true of you. And that is, we struggle. We struggle with hiding and blaming, with lust and anger. And what do the Scriptures say about the nature of who we are as a result of the fact that we lust, not just sexually, but for power, for prestige ... just for a day off? When God calls lust "adultery," and ranks anger (apart from the righteous anger in service of his glory) as serious as "murder," it isn't hyperbole. It is the gospel truth.

What is the truth for each one of us? It's easy to let our eyes pass over the words we read and quickly agree or disagree with their validity without stopping to ponder the application of those words to our lives. How do we apply the words of Jesus regarding lust and anger? How would you name your interaction with your neighbor this morning—a reflection of lust or anger? How about the strained conversation with your teenage son or daughter? The moment we allow these truths to get personal, we find it is harder to tell the truth—and harder to believe in the gospel.

> *As Christian leaders, we must see ourselves as having "leading character" that invites others to see the goodness of Christ in us.*

An extreme makeover for our character begins, then, when we embrace the gospel truth—of being marred and remade—alive in the freedom and power of the resurrection. Paul says, "I want to know Christ—yes, to know the power of his resurrection and participation in his sufferings, becoming like him in his death, and so, somehow, attaining to the resurrection from the dead" (Philippians 3:10–11). We become radically new when we bless our gifts and how God has marked our face, our story, and our calling; grieve our failings and the consequences on those we love and serve; and glory in forgiveness and live out resurrection freedom and boldness. Let's consider specifically how that can reshape the way we lead others.

Our Leadership

To have character as a leader means that you can talk about all three of these realities—being marked, marred, and remade. You can do that in the pulpit, at a staff meeting, or with colleagues one-on-one. The language you use can fit the context, rather than be spoken in the typical vernacular of religion.

I remember being at a U2 concert where the opening songs began to address the hunger of the human heart (made in God's image); then the songs moved on to expose the fact that everyone is prejudiced and envious (marred); and finally they described the hunger for a love that was all-seeing and all-embracing (remade in love). There are always innovative and unpredictable ways to reinvigorate and recast the matters of the heart. And these contexts can play a huge role in the makeover of our leading character when we are willing to get knowledge, seek prayer, grow in wisdom, and live with freedom.

Get knowledge. Nothing is harder to get than feedback from those you lead. If feedback has not been sought before, people will be reluctant to tell you the truth. If it has been done before and the data was used against others or was ignored, then, even if that happened on someone else's watch, your battle for honest feedback will be fought on an uphill slope. Leaders never get enough data about themselves—or the data they get is on either the extreme positive or extreme negative. Seldom is the data rigorous, systematic, or usable.

One of the best ways to get data on how you're doing is to hire an outside firm to orchestrate an analyzable 360-degree survey that asks a significant population of your subordinates, peers, and those to whom you report to evaluate you on many levels. Usually, the data will be anonymous and coded to help you and your organization assess your strengths and weaknesses so that you can implement change.

Other valuable data can be acquired by requesting feedback from trusted associates, friends, and family members. But simply asking, "Would you give me some feedback about what it is like to be around me or to work with me?" will result in either stunned silence or information that's so watered down it is of no value.

Instead, you have the best chance of getting useful feedback if you start the conversation by owning up to negative information everyone already knows about you. In other words, tell the truth as far as you can see it and then invite more data in that realm. As an example, I once said to a group of leaders at Mars Hill Graduate School, "I know when we get into this topic, I tend to panic. And I know that when I panic, I want to reach a quick consensus and I cut off conversation. I am not aware of other ways I handle myself at times like this. Can you help me see myself better and see what effect my behavior has on you?"

The responses I got were not easy to hear, but I took notes and did my best to clarify what each person had to say. I owned up to my failures. In addition, I built in two or three behavioral markers—or indicators—that would help me and the group recognize any reoccurrence of the same behavior. And I assured my staff that although I didn't want to derail our work again, I knew that it was likely to happen. In this way, we built plans for moving into and through my problematic behavior to a safe and productive conclusion. Doing so provided us with far more than resolution of a particular problem. It reminded us that living out the gospel, not the mere completion of a project, was the reason we had gathered.

Seek prayer. Changing the processes and techniques we use as leaders will not result in transformation—of our work worlds or of our lives. Our prime tool for a radical makeover is prayer. I have failed to apply this truth more often than I have failed in any other dimension of leadership. I simply have not breathed prayer as air, and nearly all of my most suffocating moments in leadership have come about because I didn't pray, didn't ask others to pray, or didn't listen to what prayer had to teach me. I suspect that this failure is much like facing the damage caused to oneself by smoking cigarettes and then having to ask the hard question: "Why did I allow myself to do something that I knew would harm me?"

My excuse was often, "I prayed, but I don't have the time to pray more." How often I wish I had taken more time to talk with God—up-front time that might have helped me escape the hundreds of hours it took later to resolve a crisis. I'm not saying that prayer will keep you from dealing with leadership crises, but I know this: I have faced a number of heartaches that could have been avoided had I sought more prayer from wise men and women outside of my work.

If I had, I would most likely have been called to name and deal with realities that I, instead, ignored.

I have violated (and still do, at times) what is an exceedingly obvious principle: "If you are too busy to pray, then you have even more reason to stop what you are doing and give yourself over to prayer." A transformed leader prays more desperately and more often than he or she ever did prior to experiencing a radical makeover.

Grow in wisdom. Obviously, not everything in our lives ought to be shared with our associates. While we embrace the attributes of honesty and transparency, we must do so with judgment and wisdom. I once heard about a leader who began his work in a church by sharing with the other three staff members that he often struggled with sexual lust. Within a month, a church secretary reported to the elders how uncomfortable she was working with him — not because of any inappropriate behavior, but because his revelation had created its own tension.

> *A transformed leader prays more desperately and more often than he or she ever did prior to experiencing a radical makeover.*

Disclosure takes time, restraint, and wisdom. First, we should share nothing about our lives unless it has first been vetted by the people most affected by our disclosure. Certainly, our best stories and examples often involve other people, but they are not worth telling if doing so creates heartache for these individuals. If I want to tell a story that involves my wife or children, for instance, I talk with them first. And I ask these two questions:

- Is my telling of the story true as you remember it?
- Do you feel reluctant for any reason for it to be told?

Growing in wisdom also involves understanding the implications of our disclosures in the larger context of our work. After the departure of one of our founders, I was asked by students and alumni why I had fired the person. I had not in fact fired the person, but to go into the story of this individual's departure required details that would not only violate confidentiality but also our state's personnel laws. The questions were nonstop. Explaining why I couldn't talk about the situation only created more mystery and demand to know. It was a nightmare!

Eventually, I was asked about my failure during this process, and I knew that to articulate even personal failure could become fodder for a lawsuit. The questions sent me into a flight of stonewalling. Rather than address (with ethical and legal wisdom) what could be addressed, I fled. I blamed the person who had departed, the state of Washington's personnel law, the legal system, and anyone else who happened to be lingering near the problem. In retrospect, I see that I could have simply talked about how it feels to not be able to answer. I could have engaged those who had questions in terms of the deep demand in my soul to be believed (a form of lust) and the resentment (anger) attached to my realization that nothing I could do would be enough. What I learned—too late to apply to that situation—is that we can be wise and still name what is problematic in our hearts.

As radically transformed leaders, we open ourselves up to being an example of redemption—past, present, and future. Yet our calling is also to never let those we work with forget that we are all first made beautiful in God's image and then gloriously remade in Christ's image. If all we do is confess to being marred, then we have not disclosed the truest truths about our glory. Often I find honest leaders more willing to acknowledge their failures than to confess the beautiful new heart that beats in their chests. Instead, we must disclose glory, hiding and blaming, cowardice and cruelty, and the new heart that yearns for courage and kindness.

Are you aware of why you argue against allowing your heart to be known by those you serve? Sometimes it is wise to write all those reasons on a piece of paper in order to see what patterns emerge. One pattern that will be difficult to name, at least for most of us, is the pattern of excuses that revolve around our lust to be appreciated, cared for, and respected. Another involves the contempt and withdrawal related to our anger. Until you've decoded your arguments — the ones you are conscious of (and seem so reasonable) and the deeper, more close-to-the-bone justifications — it will be nearly impossible to consider a different course of life.

Live with freedom. Too often we lose our way and find ourselves exhausted and overwhelmed with our work. Somewhere along the line, we lost our first love and the deepest impulse for why we accepted the mantle of leadership. The good news is that a radical makeover is almost always accompanied by a taste of invigoration. We need to be reminded what it means to be forgiven and set free to live with passion and joy, to be called "beloved." Then, no matter how weary and discouraged I have become, I find my heart amazed and sweetened by the privilege of leading. I am no longer aware of the burden.

A question we should ask ourselves at regular intervals is: "Am I having fun?" That question is a simple way to enter the deeper question, "Am I living in the freedom of the resurrection?" And if our answer is "no," then before we change jobs, careers, ministries, or employees, we need to ask ourselves this follow-up question:

> *As radically transformed leaders, we open ourselves up to being an example of redemption — past, present, and future.*

"Do I know the freedom of being humbled and being lifted up (see James 4:7–10) and the joy of being poor, sad, gentle, hungry, merciful, pure, peaceful, and persecuted?" (see Matthew 5:3–11). Anyone who once again answers "no" can assume that his or her heart needs to be surprised again by the gospel.

Jesus says, "And the truth will set you free" (John 8:32). He said this to people who refused to acknowledge that he spoke the truth and, instead, accused him of being demon possessed. We often call

Jesus the truth and name ourselves as his followers, and yet because the cost seems not only too severe but crazy, we refuse to live with the freedom he invites us to know. We are bound by the judgment of others; we fear the power of man more than we are grateful for the kindness of God. And so we, too, say to Jesus, "You ask me to be and to do something insane, out of the norm, and it will get me into trouble, and I don't believe in you enough to do it."

The gospel turns the world, including our own lives, upside down—which, of course, is truly right side up. Not only are we to live in freedom, but we are to offer our unique lives as an example, a picture, of the work of redemption. Not only do we *have* a character that is meant to grow more and more into the image of Jesus but we are to *be* a character who offers our unique story as a lens for others to better see the life of Jesus.

BE A CHARACTER

Once we are comfortable with what it means to have a character, the next task of a leader is to *be* a character—to be open to all the various ways God may choose to work through each of our lives.

In his elegant book on leadership, *Leading Minds*, Howard Gardner looks at how a widely diverse group of leaders—from Gandhi to Eleanor Roosevelt—led by telling stories. Their stories articulated the unnamed fears that kept them from moving forward to what they most desired, and they offered hope, invigorating others to risk creating a new world. Stories are not mere illustrations; they are the fire and blood that create the possibility of transformation. The stories that great leaders tell link the individual leader's story to the lives of those she or he serves.

Most people will not follow a leader whose life is disconnected from their own story. Think how often American politicians offer their story of humble beginnings and their status as Washington outsiders as a means to convey the promise they will bring change to the morass of politics. It is a tiresome spin that gets dismissed quickly, yet it still works well enough to secure the support of voters. Leaders, no matter what the context, must communicate their vision and plans for how they intend to journey to the desired outcome for those they serve. This can only be done well through story.

A close friend who started a financial loan business took thirty of his executives to the poverty- and violence-filled section of Montreal where he grew up in order to introduce them to the section of town that inspired his company's name. My friend, who has

> *We are to be a character who offers our unique story as a lens for others to better see the life of Jesus.*

suffered the cruelty and mockery of many for the physical disabilities related to albinism, wanted his executives to see why he values and loves his community and what it taught him about life. He invited these men and women to see, smell, and taste both heartache and hope. In addition to telling his story, he enabled his executives to see why he so prizes honesty, integrity, commitment, and risk taking. Stories shape how we see ourselves and how we envision our calling in the place we work and serve.

Every leader, no matter what the context, is a storyteller. And in telling stories we become a character in the stories of others. This friend, who took his executives on a story journey, later invited them to reflect on and write about what had motivated them to make money. He asked them to consider what they fear, what they are meant to overcome, and how their current work might be the context in which they can grow as people and not merely secure their financial futures.

In sharing his story, he helped his executives reflect on their own stories. The loan company is committed to making money, yet the culture established by this leader also provides significant sums to those who work with the homeless. By introducing his executives to the homeless and offering a means of partnering with the passions of their own hearts to give back to their world, he has become a character in their stories. A leader must *be* a character to lead others to greater "leading character."

Some Real Characters

Being a character is as old as time, and the Bible is filled with stories about individuals who were only too human — real characters — and yet were used by God in powerful ways. As we acknowledged earlier, the Bible is not reluctant to tell the stories of highly flawed and, at times, outright ridiculously failed human beings. Consider the life and story of our father of faith, Abraham.

God calls Abram to leave his home and country without telling him why he is leaving or where he is going. He obeys God. Yet within the same chapter that describes his departure (Genesis 12), he lies and tells Pharaoh's representatives that his wife, Sarai, is really his sister. He gets them all in big trouble. God has promised that Abram will be the father of a mighty nation that will bless all people. Yet when pregnancy doesn't occur, he allows his wife to talk him into taking a concubine to bear his child. It is a disastrous choice, and, eventually, he has to run off his son Ishmael and Ishmael's mother, Hagar, to keep peace with his wife.

As Abraham and Sarah, bearing the new names given them by God, age and get beyond the expected years of childbearing, God sends a messenger to tell them they will have a son. Abraham laughs and then Sarah mocks the news. After this, in another bizarre flight from the truth, Abraham goes back to an old lie and creates new havoc by telling King Abimelech that Sarah is his sister. In his defense to the king, he basically says, "Well, I figured this to be a godless place ... besides she is my sister — we both have the same father, though different mothers — and I married her" (see Genesis 20:11–12).

Abraham *blames* Abimelech's kingdom and then *hides* behind a technical truth while obscuring the fact that he is married to Sarah.

This is the father of our faith—not such a great lineage, we might think. Yet, he is God's chosen leader to establish the people of God, Israel, and to bless the earth. Go figure.

Was there no one more righteous than Abraham, or Jacob, or Moses, or David? Jacob was a deceiver; Moses lost his way to the Promised Land because of his anger; and the apple of God's eye, David, was an adulterer and a murderer. It gives me pause to wonder why God called *me* into leadership. But then, I've been known to be a character myself.

Gone Fishin'

I have been amazed at how God uses the various foibles of my human nature to work in and through me. In the spirit of transparency I've been advocating, let me tell a story to illustrate my point.

A number of years ago, I had the privilege of sitting at lunch with a good friend who looked directly at me in the midst of our conversation and uttered these words: "You concern me because you're a very boring man."

How was I supposed to respond to something like that? "Uh, pass the salt. I'll try to spice up my life for you."

What I actually said was, "What are you saying?"

"You work too much," he said.

When I pressed him about his concern, he responded, "You have no hobbies. You take no breaks. You have no Sabbath. You don't take time off."

"Well, what do you suggest?"

"I want to take you fishing."

Say, what? To me, fishing meant holding a pole with a line going into the water. That line has a little red and white bulb attached that sits on the top, while the rest of it hangs below with a hook that has something dead on the end of it. And you hold onto that, being as still and quiet as possible, while you wait for something to happen.

His concern was boredom? Personally, I'd rather be locked in a closet!

I expressed these concerns and he said, "No, no, no, you don't understand. I want to take you *fly*-fishing."

A Wade in the Water

Well, I'd seen the movie *A River Runs Through It*. I knew fly-fishing meant wading into water and swinging the line out and back, and I could picture the beauty of the water and the rocks that surround this activity. I figured I could try anything moral once, and so, yeah, I went fishing. And within the first few minutes, my friend had taught me some of the little basics—enough for me to know that this really was going to be fun.

I just moved the line back and forth, back and forth. But about the third time I had it back, as I began to go forward, it wouldn't budge. I turned around and my friend had this look of astonishment mixed with horror and pain. I had hooked him in the ear! And he was right—fly-fishing was not boring! I got to take the hook out and do a little surgery.

I got into fly-fishing; I *really* got into it. I bought all the gear. (I didn't realize how much I'd enjoy gear. Now I understand that gear is to men what jewelry is to women.) I began to look at magazines and think about things like rods, reels, and waders.

Montana Mayhem

Around the time that I began fly-fishing, I received an invitation to teach at a Bible conference in Montana—and if you know anything about Montana, you know it's Mecca for people who fly-fish. So when I got this invitation, my answer came quickly and easily. It didn't require prayer ... it didn't require asking God's will ... I just said, "Yes!" I even took the additional step of inviting my wife and my ten-year-old son Andrew to accompany me.

The first day we were there, I didn't have to teach. So about 8:00 p.m., I went into the water with a float tube and all my gear. I was so excited! It was dusk and the mountains were beautiful. This was a wonderful, exhilarating break to be able to fly-fish before I was to teach the next morning.

I walked into the water, and although the beauty surrounding me as the sun began to set was the center of my attention, I couldn't help but notice that there were many birds flying around me. I'm really not an outdoorsy-type person and I don't know much about ornithology, but still, the presence of these birds surprised me. I guess I thought they would be in bed by then.

But they were fully awake, flying very rapidly as they went right over me, up and around me. And I thought, "Gosh, these birds are unusual." Suddenly, I realized they weren't birds. They were bats! And I am *terrified* of bats!

I started using my rod as a tool to create what I would call a No-Fly Zone. And as I was swinging my rod about—let's see, how should I tell you this?—you know how you always hear that you cannot hit a bat? Well, it's not true. I hit a bat. And it dropped into the water just a few feet from me.

At that point, I was horrified because I'd actually smacked a bat into the water. Then, as it surfaced, there was this moment—this very *intense* moment—in which this bat and I looked right at each other. Although I can't speak bat language, I had the sense that the bat was looking at me and thinking something like, "Look! An island!" as it began to move in my direction.

Well, there I was in my float tube, trying to move away from this creature. But it could swim much faster than I could move. Okay, I'm not proud of what I'm about to describe, but I have to say ... it was self-defense.

I whacked the bat!

The first whack didn't work, so I whacked it again and again because it kept coming and coming. So I kept hitting at it and finally—this is horrifying to admit—I drowned one of God's creatures.

By this time, I was completely panicked. I wanted *out* of there. But at that moment, all of a sudden, a fish that had been created from the foundation of the earth for this very moment came and took my fly!

You might think that would be exciting. But I didn't *want* to catch a fish; I just wanted out of that water. So I reeled in as fast as I could, with no thought of playing this fish. I wanted it *in* so I could get *out*.

I must also tell you that up to this point, all I had ever caught were trout—sweet, small, beautifully colored trout. As I pulled this fish up, it became clear this was no trout. It was a big, ugly gray fish, and its huge mouth was opened very wide. I was startled!

I don't like to touch fish, but I had to get that big fish off the hook. Again, I can't explain it, but I just had kind of a meltdown. I tried to shake the fish off the hook, but I couldn't. I wanted out of the water so badly that I began swinging the fish. In fact, I swung that fish so hard that eventually I ... forgive me ... I ripped off its lips, which sent it hurtling back into the water.

I was out of there in nothing flat. It was dark by then, and I hurried to the dock and climbed up. Then, as I was walking toward the shore with all my equipment, I noticed a figure sitting on a chair about fifty feet away, near the end of the dock. As I got closer, I could tell it was a man—an older gentleman—and I started hoping I could just walk by him quickly.

Let me interrupt this story with a word from our sponsor. It may seem like a terrible time to break into the narrative, but I want to make sure you remember what I've asked you to consider in this chapter. Why did I want to walk by quickly? I didn't want to be seen. I didn't want to speak. I didn't want to make face-to-face contact with this man. I knew he'd just witnessed the entire bat-drowning-fish-ripping fiasco—which meant I'd been exposed as a complete failure as a fisherman. All I wanted to do was hide. It's one thing to say you're the worst of all sinners in a dignified public setting; it's much worse to be caught looking foolish by a stranger.

If you were to survey the major stories in my life—how I came to know Jesus, went to seminary, met my wife, got into ministry, pursued my education, and became part of a new graduate school—you would see certain issues that mark my life thematically. I have stories of shame, odd coincidence, violence, cowardly flight, and surly fight, and stories of sweet redemption that bring hope to my heart. How have these stories shaped me, molded me, and engraved my character for ill and for good? How do I tell these stories? We must look diligently at how all our stories have marked us and ask God: "How am I to use this engraving for your glory—where am I to serve, whom am I to serve, and how am I to serve in order to follow the marking you have worked into my story?" Was I being sensitive when I fired that employee who needed three firing conversations? Somewhat, maybe. But I was far more committed to having that man like me, and to think positively of me, than I was to be clear, concise, and, in one sense, to honor him in the process. We hide. We blame.

And that's exactly what I wanted to do on that dock. But as I walked by this man, he reached up and grabbed my arm. Then he pulled me down close to his face, and said, "Son, I've been fishing for over fifty years. I want you to know I have never seen the likes of this. And I just wanted to thank you."

I'm usually a pretty good communicator, but I had no words for that gentleman. And for the next several days at the conference, I avoided him.

If you're a teacher or leader, you know what it is to be in front of an audience when someone is sitting there who doesn't like you, who has spoken words against you, who questions your leadership, who doubts your sincerity, who has questioned your character in ways that have caused you pain. You know what it is like to have someone in your world who, as you see them, provokes all the questions you have about yourself, about God, about your work, about your leadership. I don't know what you do in those situations, but here's what I do: I avoid them.

And for the rest of the conference, I did my best to avoid this man who had seen me in the water. He sat right in front when I taught, but

I moved my eyes up and around him. At meals, I ate on the other side of the dining hall. For a few days, I managed to keep him at bay.

Each day of the conference, I took my son fishing for a couple hours right after lunch. For three days straight, we caught nothing.

It's one thing to say you're the worst of all sinners in a dignified public setting; it's much worse to be caught looking foolish by a stranger.

On that third day, as we were coming in, getting the boat secured and all the equipment back to our cabin, the gentleman I'd been avoiding pursued me. I could see him coming, out of the corner of my eye, and I knew I couldn't get everything done quickly enough to flee—which would have been too obvious anyway, even for me. When he got to me, he said, "I see you've been taking your son out to catch fish."

"Yes, sir, I have."

"I noticed you've been taking him out between one and three-thirty each day."

"Yes, sir."

"Also noticed you haven't caught anything."

"Yes, sir."

"Do you know that fish don't usually bite between one and three-thirty?"

"No, sir, I didn't know that."

"You don't know much about fishing, do you?"

"No, sir, I don't."

"Do you want your boy to catch a fish?"

"Absolutely. Yes."

"Then what I want you to do is be out here at five-thirty tomorrow morning."

He gave me two good lures and told me a few specific places to fish, information I did not have and would not have had if he had not spoken into my life—if he had not, in his own way, been an angel of confrontation, of information, of exposure. Had he not, in some

74

sense, entered what a marred reality I reveal about Jesus Christ, I would never have known what I was doing wrong.

Just One More Cast

The next morning, Andrew and I went out at five-thirty. We were so excited. I had a sense that today would finally be the day. We fished from five-thirty to seven-thirty, but neither of us caught a thing. I had told my wife we'd be back at eight o'clock, so about seven forty-five, I looked at my son and said, "We've gotta go. We've got to go in."

"Oh, Dad, please, just let me fish a little bit more."

My first thought, though I didn't voice it, was, *What for? What for!*

And, although this was not one of the most profound issues in the world, I was ticked at God. Ticked at the fact that he could divide the Red Sea, but he wouldn't provide my son with one lousy fish—just because he has a father who's incompetent and doesn't know how to fish or where to go or what to do. I was furious with God, and there was a part of me, at that moment, that hated hope. I hated the prospect of looking at my son, knowing how much he wanted to catch a fish, and knowing that it was not going to happen.

With that thought, I looked at him and said, "No, we need to go."

He looked at me plaintively and very quietly said, "Please, Dad, just one more time?"

Inside, I was raging. Nevertheless, I looked at my son and answered with words tempered by a message the Spirit of God had, in just that instant, spoken to me: *Do you want to kill hope in him? Do you want to kill hope in your son as you've allowed it, in this moment, to be killed in you?*

I softened. Who knows how it occurred, but I softened. I looked at my son and I said, "No, Andrew, you cannot fish *one* more time. But you can fish *five* more."

He looked at me with that look, like, "Really?"

"Yes," I said. "Not four, not six, *five.*"

The first cast went out. Then the second. And the third. With each cast I prayed, "Oh, Lord, please let him have a fish!" By the fourth cast, I was back to thinking, *Why should I hope? Yeah, you suckered me into dreaming for my son again. I hoped again—and my hopes were dashed.*

I turned away from my son and began to pull on the oars as Andrew threw his line out for the fifth time. All of a sudden he was yelling, "Dad! Stop!"

I turned around and saw that his pole was bent over. "Andrew, move your rod around a little bit."

As he moved the pole around, I could see there was no movement on the line. "You've snagged a log or you've got a boot," I said, "but you don't have a fish." I turned back to the oars, but a moment later he yelled again, "Dad, look!"

This time I saw that now the line was moving. His rod was bent and it was moving! For the next five or six minutes, Andrew fought to bring in his fish. Soon we could see that he didn't have a beautiful mountain trout—what he had on his line was a northern pike! (I don't know if you've ever seen a northern pike, but they look downright satanic!)

As he fought to reel in the fish, I could tell Andrew was getting tired. At one point I said to him, "Andrew, let me hold the rod, just for a moment."

He looked at me and, probably thinking of my bat meltdown, said, "Like you did the other night?" I didn't know whether to laugh or cry.

When he finally got the fish up next to the boat, he said, "Dad, grab it!"

I looked at him and said, "It's *your* fish." (Hey, turnaround is fair play.)

We got his fish off the hook and rowed back to shore. It was a phenomenal moment. It was probably one of the most important moments, ever, in my life as a father. Then, perhaps one of the most important moments in my son's life took place as we neared the shore, when he said, quietly, "Dad, we have a God, don't we?"

I looked at him. "Yeah. Yeah, we do."

Another moment passed and he looked up at me. "Dad, I know God's name."

I had never heard him talk about the name of God other than, of course, the Bible names he had learned as a kid. "What do you mean, Andrew?"

"I know God's name."

"What is his name for you?"

What he said was, "God's name is 'the God of the fifth cast.'"

The more you tell the truth about yourself ... the more effective your leadership will become, the more you will develop a true leading character.

About four months later, that translated for him into coming to know Jesus Christ as his Lord and Savior.

Now, as I write this story, more than a decade has passed. My son is a brilliant, almost supernatural fisherman. It would be wrong for me to leave the impression that from this memorable fishing trip on, life has been smooth for us. It hasn't been. He has struggled in his faith, at times, and has fought and distanced himself from his father. But I have not forgotten a significant moment of redemption for me, for him, and for us. Nor has he. When we each have lost hope again that God would be God, the story has served not merely as encouragement but as a warning: "Do not forget the Lord your God," and we have been called to return to the fish that God so kindly brought to the surface.

Leading Character

Where did Andrew's insight come from? My faithfulness in teaching? My faithfulness of making the Scriptures clear to him? In one sense, yes. But far more, it came, in many ways, in the midst of my own humiliation, my own exposure, and my own propensity to blame God and others. Do you see that it is in the midst of bearing God's mark, his character, and of being marred by our own sin (and being willing to name that for our world rather than hiding from it) that God not only works to redeem us, but he works through us to reach others?

Too often we think sharing our weaknesses will cause us to lose respect. We think making our weaknesses known will cause us to lose the honor to be able to proclaim the Word of God in our congregations or our businesses. I no longer believe that is true. Not today, in our postmodern culture. What I do believe is the more you tell the truth about yourself—appropriately, winsomely, age-appropriately, within a context—the more effective your leadership will become, the more you will develop a true leading character. The more you tell of your own failure of character, the more God will use that for his purposes.

Do you see the handiwork of God in your story? We may never fully understand why we were given an alcoholic father or a distant and angry mother. We may never fully see God's deepest desire for our suffering or our blessings, yet we are intended to bless God for how he has written our life for his glory. What would it mean for you to bless the parts of your story that bear sorrow and joy, death and life?

Let us become people who can confess we are sinners. And when we do, what will be the effect? What will be the results for each of us?

REVEALING GOD'S CHARACTER

Despite the fact that the movie *Chariots of Fire* is nearly three decades old, there is a scene that many people still know by heart. As I speak before groups of various size and makeup, I enjoy asking the question, "When Eric Liddell said, 'I believe God made me for a purpose, but he also made me fast. And when I run I feel his ...' what did he say?" Members of the audience nearly always joyfully respond, "Pleasure!" People remember this line because, in many respects, it is the key message of the film; the object of God's delight was clear. We experience God's delight, God's pleasure, when we do what he created us to do.

What do you do that most gives you a sense of God's delight? What brings you delight? This is a question designed to move you closer to determining what unique aspects of your life contribute most to revealing God's character. If you're a leader, then I hope leading is close to the top of your list—otherwise, you likely will not thrive or perhaps even survive your leadership experience.

Several years ago, I sat with a friend at breakfast and we talked with some seriousness about our lives. This man is a generous, peaceful presence, and he is often invited to teach in wildly diverse settings. He hates conflict, but has had to stand against a leader who has turned against one of his dear friends.

God loves to use our strengths to get us into battle. In my friend's case, his peace-making skills are well known and the basis for his being invited to mediate a contentious situation. The mediation required him to enter into a conflict that he would have preferred to avoid. But while God uses our strengths to get us into battle, he also uses our weaknesses for his glory—to not only change others but to transform us as well. Through the conflict, God gently exposed my friend's tendency to flee and hide, which is his refusal to be strong, and called him to be a warrior for his friend against the leader who was involved.

During the course of our conversation, my friend pointed out that, unlike him, I am far more ready for a fight, more open to conflict, and far less apt to hide. I told him of the situation God had put me in at that time, which was to not fight but to stand and see that the battle was God's, not mine. My friend reminded me of the passage in 2 Chronicles 20 where the warriors were told not to fight but to allow the choir to go before them and sing. As they sang, God routed the three armies that were about to destroy the people of God. God wanted me to avoid the fight; he wanted my friend to go to war.

In a similar way, we are each called by God to bring our strengths to the battle, and yet it is through our weaknesses that he intends to redeem us, our organizations, and our people (see 2 Corinthians 12:8–10). And when God redeems, it is his character that is made known through the transformation of our own character. There is no delight in life that is meant to be greater or sweeter than making known the heart of God through a humble and beautiful life. The effect is something remarkable on the inside and on the outside.

Remarkable on the Inside

Nothing is more thrilling than to see someone progress from simply following Christ to becoming a committed disciple. As the word *disciple* implies, there is a willingness, in this new role, not merely to hear and consider Christ's words but to submit to them and to take on his yoke as our own. It is the cry of Paul who says, "I want to know Christ—yes, to know the power of his resurrection and participation in his sufferings" (Philippians 3:10). In essence, he is saying, "I want power and I want intimacy." Paul is crying out for strength and tenderness—in different words, yet with the same desire to reveal God's good character. Transformation creates a deeper and more refined desire for the heart of God, the result of which will be greater gratitude, truth, and boldness.

Gratitude

If you're the worst of sinners, then you can relate personally to the words Jesus speaks to the woman in Luke 7: "But whoever has been forgiven little loves little" (v. 47). That's because you know the other side of that equation is equally true: Whoever is forgiven much, loves much. And why, when you're the worst of sinners, do you love so much? Because you're so grateful!

In my experience, nothing chips away at gratitude more than the daily grind of leadership: the crises, confusion, conflicts, loneliness, and exhaustion. As leaders, we're sometimes amazed we're even able to get out of bed on certain mornings! We do, but do we do so with gratitude? Not the gratitude that comes when a problem is resolved, but gratitude that no matter how the issue plays out, we have the opportunity to be molded and shaped into a more glorious image of the person of Christ.

Gratitude deepens desire. The more grateful we are—the more our heart sings with the praise of beauty, goodness, and truth—the more we are seized by the small moments of grace that we "important" people are often too busy to see. It is true that the rich get richer. In this case, a wealth of gratitude sharpens our senses, making us increasingly able to take in the glories God has scattered throughout the world for us to find. No one is richer than those who are grateful.

Can you recall a significant battle you were called to fight years ago—one you presumed might destroy you? Do you recall the worry, the late nights, the strategic plans you made, and how it all went far worse than you could have dreamt in a nightmare? Did it burn away some of the dross? Did it mark you with scars worthy of revealing the suffering of Christ? In retrospect, do you bless that suffering and what it called you to become?

If not, then there may well be pockets of ingratitude—what we might typically call bitterness—that still reside in your heart. What you went through is still there, inviting you to look closely at your failure of tenderness or strength. It is there to expose your habit of hiding or blaming. It is a window to help you look at your own struggle with lust and anger. In spite of all that has been left unaddressed, God has chosen to work through you and to bless you. Imagine how many more opportunities he will have to do that once your heart is amazed that he calls you beloved and that you are known as fully as you can be known. It is time to allow fresh air to pour through those hidden places and to know forgiveness, wonder, and gratitude.

Truth
If I'm the worst of sinners and I know I have no right or reason by competence or knowledge to be the president of my organization—

no more so than you do to be a pastor, a parent, or the owner of your business—then the reality is this: It is in our brokenness that we have our greatest opportunity to reveal the heart of God's goodness. Will we take that opportunity? Will we tell the truth?

If we tell the *truth*, here is the fundamental point: The worst is already known about us. What *worse* is there to know?

When we understand that the worst is already known, that offers us tremendous freedom to tell our stories and freedom, in our daily life, to reveal the character of God. Such conversations can take place on a plane. You can share your story as you interact over a cup of coffee.

The next time someone asks you, "What do you do for a living?" answer them: "I'm a storyteller with one story worth telling. Let me tell you about ..."

Okay, you likely will never say those words, but there are a thousand ways of launching into your story that will make sense to the person, group, or audience you address. The next time someone complains to you about their spouse, their work, or their life, resist the urge to merely say, "Hey, me too." We can all do far, far better.

For starters, we can ask hard questions, but only if we are willing to answer those same questions ourselves. We can invite people to tell their stories as fully as they desire. We can inquire about matters that they only hint at but don't name, whether it involves work, or faith, or a personal issue. Doing so needn't take the form of barging in. Instead, begin by asking for permission: "Jack, you mentioned that things are not good with your wife. I'm not a marriage counselor, but I have known, and at times still know, great heartache with my wife. We also know great sweetness and hope. I don't want to blow off your remark about whether you two are going to make it, but I also don't know if I have permission to ask you more. Do you want me to step into these issues with you?"

Making such an offer may launch a process that will consume many hours (weeks, months) of your time. It may generate real sorrow and pain as you identify with your friend's situation. The payoff, however, can be great, because when combined with gratitude, truth will always birth greater boldness in our lives.

Boldness

The more grateful I am—when the worst is already known about me—then I am, indeed, free to fail. I'm free to take risks. Ultimately, I'm free to not worry, in one sense, about the consequences. I'm free to take the bold steps needed as a leader. I am free to make the difficult decisions required of me as a leader. I am free to reveal both my strength and my tenderness. Why? Because if everything is a gift, then, fundamentally, we need not fear loss.

A dear friend, in the middle of a contentious and highly politicized power struggle with his church board, took a bold and unexpected stand. For years, one elder had bullied the board to vote his way by threatening to quit the church and take with him the 20 percent of the church's finances contributed by his extended family.

Even my friend came under attack. That elder had vigorously opposed my friend's selection as senior pastor, but lost. In the job interview, my friend disclosed to the board that he had struggled with alcoholism in his earlier years. He had sought treatment and had over a decade of sobriety. If the board hired him, he didn't want them to later be surprised by this information.

Soon after, subtle and vicious rumors began. My friend endured the assaults. He addressed the accusations in public. He lived out what it means to love one's enemies. But in an effort to avoid conflict, he at times failed to speak his mind and vote in a manner consistent with his conscience.

After several years, the powerful elder again threatened to resign. This time the rest of the board gleefully accepted. My friend disagreed. He said if the elder were to resign, it should not be in that context. He then admitted that he too had become bitter and resentful, believing the elder was the basis for the rumor nightmare that he and his family had endured. Confessing that he was wrong, he asked for the elder's forgiveness.

The board was stunned. One elder said, "Until we deal with our own failure and learn to make decisions without the fear of his departure, we are no better."

The story doesn't have a smooth Christian sit-com ending. A few elders resigned. The powerful elder sneered at the cowards and remained on the board. But now, due to my friend's bold courage in a drama of repentance, new board members serve with a sense of integrity and joy, making decisions without the shadow of fear and regret.

The reality is that both the blessings and sorrows of this life are a gift. And if I am to welcome hardship as a friend and make a place for it in my heart to serve the greater purposes of God, then will I pray for boldness as the apostle Paul did? Paul prayed for boldness more often than he made any other request.

Will you pray for boldness in using your story? If you're a pastor with abuse in your past, will you use the story? Do you understand how many people in this world have never heard the words "sexual abuse" from a pulpit despite the fact that some 60 percent of women and in the range of 38 percent of men struggle with a history of such trauma? Why is that not being named? Are we aware there is spousal abuse in many congregations? Do we name that?

Do we own up to the fact that instead of dealing directly with someone at work, we go to someone else and gossip, conducting a guerrilla war against the person we dislike? Almost every work environment permits and utilizes collusion. We go to someone else to complain about a coworker. We don't speak directly to the coworker. And if someone is complaining to us about a coworker, we listen and then add a line or two about our own discontent. Collusion, like gossip, is a dark means of creating cohesion in subgroups, yet it can ruin an organization faster than a competitor's strategy to take away one's market share.

Can we name our darkness? Why should we? Because as people who have been there, we are the ones with the greatest sense of hope that redemption truly does redeem.

Indeed, then, if we're grateful, we can risk. And if we can risk, the promise is this: We will be more open and more honest. We will be freer. And the result of that, I believe, is that we'll become bolder, happier people. What an odd thing: Darkness leads to joy. Truth leads to a greater truth. Where have we heard this before?

Remarkable on the Outside

The bottom line, then, is this: If we want to be people who transform our worlds, it will begin when we describe the *character* of our story as an *absence of character* that's being redeemed by a *great character*, and that is the God of the universe. How do we begin? Let me tell you a story.

A friend asked if I would preach in his church. I said, "Yes, but why would you pay me to fly all the way across the country just to preach one time?" He explained that a conflict had arisen among his elders that he believed would be resolved only if they were willing to name their own failures before they addressed the weighty decision burdening them. "I want you to preach on owning up to being an adulterer and murderer from Matthew 5." I laughed. "You want to pay me to come in and tell the truth about myself so your elders might face what you are unable to say to them?" He laughed and admitted, "If I preached what you will say, I'd be in major trouble."

I was honored, but saddened. I told him I would do it, but for far more money than he had intended to pay, explaining that the wages of a "prophet" were simply higher than the pay of a preacher.

What is required to begin this truth-telling revolution? Like my friend who invited me to preach, we have to admit there is a problem, and the truth needs to be known and told. And that requires that we ask others to offer us the truth about ourselves and our organization.

Get Data That Is Irrefutable

I am amazed at how few organizations set aside the time and finances to take a good look at themselves. The best way I know to do this is through a review that surveys the organization from top to bottom, creating data the organization can use as part of its strategic planning and job evaluations. Unfortunately, one of the least-reviewed sectors in America is the local church. This, despite the fact that there are different groups that could provide valuable insights if they were surveyed, including the pastoral staff, administration, elders/deacons, lay leaders, volunteers, congregation, visitors, people who have come and left after a few visits, long-term involved attendees who have left unhappy, and others in the community who know of the church but don't attend. How do people perceive your work? Do those who serve understand your mission? Are attendees growing in their faith? It is impossible to make changes—or, at least, the right changes—and to measure your success if you don't know where you are right now.

Once you have the data, it is important to take sufficient time to digest it, personally and corporately, an activity in which a wise consultant can be a resource worth his or her weight in gold. Your consultant can offer a neutral, objective perspective and can assist you in not only digesting the information but in planning how best to communicate and implement the changes related to the findings.

You will also want to consider and digest what you learn elsewhere, including the information you've read here. A word of caution: Don't read this material one week and decide to "go tell the truth" the next week, at the first opportunity to "get it off your chest." For your information to be effective, thoughtful preparation is required.

Get Data That Is Personal

To begin a major enterprise of data collection, reflection, and change requires a long-term strategy. To begin on a more limited basis, ask just three people who know you to give you feedback. How do you determine which people to ask? First, what three individuals do you trust?

Let me assume one will be your spouse. (If it is not your spouse, then there are other issues that likely need to be addressed.) Second, pick a good friend unrelated to your work. And third, pick a trusted and confidential partner within your organization. Separately, ask all three these simple questions, to be answered in writing and returned to you before you meet. This builds on the work described earlier and takes a more personal look at your life.

- Describe for me a time when you felt: "I am so privileged to know you."
- Describe for me a situation when you thought: "He/she is so blind I can't believe it."
- In what situations would you assume I am most likely not going to tell the truth?
- In what moments do you feel most confident that I will rise to the occasion and handle a situation well?

Here is one way to use the data: give your trusted three people the questions, get their written feedback, meet with them one on one, ponder the data by journaling and praying, and then meet with the three of them together. Depending on the individuals involved and your receptivity to their feedback, this informal group may be as powerful and motivating as any consultant and as informative as the facts found in a more organized data-crunching process. Take the time and space to ponder what you have learned. Such a process might seem excessive, but if you are going to do this much work, then you might as well complete the whole marathon.

Allow Data about Your Dignity and Depravity to Amaze You

As you review the information, you will recognize a myriad of possibilities for change. But hold off on any actions until you have taken the time to be amazed—in awe of both your depravity and your dignity. We are meant to see the reality of our depravity as awe-full, provoking us to plead for mercy that is bountiful and free. We are also meant to experience the work of God in developing the goodness of our character as awe-some, prompting us to praise God.

Amazement is, in fact, better ground for transformation of character than mere action could ever be. Are you amazed? Are you humbled? I suspect both, and further, that you will be humbled because what you heard is as much about how wonderful it is to be in a relationship with you as how hard it is to deal with some elements of your character.

A simple rule of leadership is that we can never ask anyone to go any further than we are willing to go. If we labor for others' transformation of character, we must be the first to be transformed. If we want others to tell the truth, we must go first.

In the movie *We Were Soldiers Once ... and Young*, Colonel Moore, the commanding officer, was the first boot to hit the battleground and, at the deeply moving end of the film, the last boot to leave the Vietnam battlefield where many of his men had died. During the height of the battle, someone back at headquarters demanded he leave the near certain massacre of his men. He refused and instead kept the promise he had made to be the first on the ground and the last to leave. He kept his word. Our task as leading characters is no different.

As a true leading character, my boot must strike the ground first and I must say, "This is a true saying, and everyone should believe it: Christ Jesus came into the world to save sinners—and I was the worst one of all" (see 1 Timothy 1:15). And I need to be the last boot off the ground, saying the same words, after the battle has ended.

When I am prone to quit, which seems far more often than is reasonable for a leading character, I find myself returning time and again to the last chapter in the last book Paul wrote before he was executed. He is in prison, cold and alone. And as he reflects on his life and the near certainty of his death, he says this:

> As for me, my life has already been poured out as an
> offering to God. The time of my death is near. I have

fought the good fight, I have finished the race, and I have remained faithful. And now the prize awaits me—the crown of righteousness, which the Lord, the righteous Judge, will give me on the day of his return. And the prize is not just for me but for all who eagerly look forward to his appearing.

— *2 Timothy 4:6–8 NLT*

The day of death will come for each of us. And I know all of us long to be able to say we have fought the good fight, finished the race, and done so faithfully. Paul did so because he knew no one needed grace more than he did; no one was more in need of forgiveness. The prize for those who finish is the crown of righteousness that is summed up in the phrase, "Welcome home, my good and faithful servant."

Are you amazed? Are you humbled?

The more we allow our hearts to hear with strength and courage, tenderness and mercy, the more we will be amazed at how God has worked in us and longs to continue the good work he has begun.

We must be the first to say that we need transformation and the last to say it is finished. Such a leader I wish to become; such is a leader I'd follow to storm the gates of hell.

May that be true of all who lead with a true leading character.

CHAPTER THREE

Overcoming Your
Shadow Mission

John Ortberg

Everybody—every human being on earth—has a mission. We were all put here for a purpose. Organizations like businesses, churches, and schools have them too. Leaders love to think about mission, love to cast vision for the mission, love to strategize about mission, love to achieve mission, love to celebrate mission.

And everybody has a *shadow mission*. Our lives, and the lives of the groups we're part of, can drift into the pursuit of something unworthy and dark. To give in to our shadow mission is—or should be—our greatest fear. To overcome our shadow mission is what this chapter is about. But I'm getting ahead of the story.

A few years ago a friend talked me into going on one of those discover-the-wild-inner-hairy-warrior-within-you men's weekends. It was held at a remote and primitive quasi-military campground. I could tell you where it was, but then I'd have to kill you. We arrived in darkness. Silent men with flashlights who had watched *Apocalypse Now* once too often led us wordlessly to a processing room. Our duffel bags were searched, and all prohibited items (snacks, reading materials, signal flares) were confiscated. We were assigned numbers that were to be used instead of our names to identify us through most of the weekend.

We chanted. We marched unclad through the snow. For two days we ate bark and berries. We were sleep deprived. We howled at the moon. We sat on our haunches in a Chippewa warrior teepee/sauna purifying our souls in the glandular fellowship of sweat, thirty men evaporating in a space no more than six sane Chippewa warriors would have tried to crowd into.

Without an authentic mission, we will be tempted to drift on autopilot, to let our lives center around something that is unworthy, something selfish, something dark — a shadow mission.

But strangely enough, in the middle of all the psychobabble and melodrama came moments of unforgettable insight. One of the topics we covered at this retreat was how we were created for a mission. This was familiar territory. Then one speaker said something that stuck with me. He said if we don't embrace our true mission, we will by default pursue what he called a "shadow mission"—patterns of thought and action based on temptations and our own selfishness that lead us to betray our deepest values. The result: regret and guilt.

He told us what his particular shadow mission consists of: "My shadow mission is to watch TV and masturbate while the world goes to hell."

His language was more raw than this, and a round of nervous laughter swept across the circle of men.

"I'm going to say it one more time," the man said, "only this time I want you to listen and not laugh." And he said it again: "My shadow mission is to watch TV and masturbate while the world goes to hell."

Silence.

Each of us was thinking the same thing: how easily any of our lives can slide into such a self-centered, trivial pursuit. This guy wasn't tempted to be Adolf Hitler or Saddam Hussein. He would have fought against that kind of outright evil. It was the banality of his shadow mission that made it so possible.

I had never heard the phrase before. I had never named what my shadow mission might be. But I understood. I knew.

You and I were created to have a mission in life. We were made to make a difference. But if we do not pursue the mission for which God designed and gifted us, we will find a substitute. We cannot live in the absence of purpose. Without an authentic mission, we will be tempted to drift on autopilot, to let our lives center around something that is unworthy, something selfish, something dark — a shadow mission.

Later on we will learn how to identify and battle both our own shadow missions and the shadow missions of the organizations or teams we lead. But for now I want to underscore just how serious this topic is. When our lives deteriorate into the pursuit of a shadow mission, the world loses. Shadow missions are what we foolishly pursue "while the world goes to hell."

You may scoff at the idea that your shadow mission has any bearing on the larger world. Our eyes remain veiled to the ultimate consequences of our choices. But the Bible tells many stories in which God reveals what the bitter end can be of a shadow mission: death. And the joyous reward of fighting that shadow mission: life. We now turn to one of the classic stories.

SHADOW MISSIONS OF EPIC PROPORTION

The book of Esther is, among other things, an epic story of missions and shadow missions and how they are woven into the great mission of God. Each character in the story has a choice between a mission and a shadow mission. And as they choose, destinies are formed and the world is changed. We'll look at four characters in particular: King Xerxes, Esther, Haman, and Mordecai.

King Xerxes

Our first character is King Xerxes. His kingdom extended over 127 provinces, from Asia Minor all the way down into Africa, then across to northern parts of India. Although Xerxes was immensely powerful, he was not an admirable character. The writer of Esther uses skill, satire, and exaggeration to give us a picture of an ostentatious king who wants to show off his greatness but in fact has no inner strength of character and constantly needs other people to help him make up his mind.

The story begins with the king at a 180-day banquet—six months of serious partying (three banquets are described in the first chapter alone; one way to divide the book up is as a series of banquets). As the writer puts it, "For a full 180 days [Xerxes] displayed the vast wealth of his kingdom and the splendor and glory of his majesty" (Esther 1:4).

Following that feast, King Xerxes throws another party for the whole capital that is open to common people. The text says, "Wine was served in goblets of gold, each one different from the other, and the royal wine was abundant, in keeping with the king's liberality. By the king's command each guest was allowed to drink with no restrictions, for the king instructed all the wine stewards to serve each man what he wished" (1:7–8). No restrictions, no restraint, unlimited, and everyone drinks from uniquely designed goblets of gold.

On the seventh day, "when King Xerxes was in high spirits from wine" (1:10), he sends for the queen, Vashti. He has been showing off his possessions; now he wants to show off his ultimate possession, his wife.

What do you think he wants to show them about her? Her brains? "Vashti, darling, why don't you come and entertain my guests by solving some math problems." Her sense of humor? "Vashti, tell us some jokes!" No, he wants Vashti to come "in order to display her beauty to the people and nobles, for she was lovely to look at" (1:11).

Then an extraordinary thing happens. Vashti says no: *Come parade myself before a drunken mob after seven days of Miller time?*

I don't think so. She says thanks very much but she would just as soon take a pass and stay home to wash her hair.

You would think the king might realize what an awkward position he put her in, but you'd be wrong. "Then the king became furious and burned with anger" (1:12). Vashti has threatened his shadow mission of impressing a nation. She has made him look weak, and that always provokes a deeply emotional response.

So Xerxes turns to experts in matters of law and justice — their version of the Supreme Court. He can't control the queen, so he makes this a matter of state: "What am I going to do about my wife?" he asks his experts. "I can't do a thing with her. If word gets out about this, then all the wives will rebel against their husbands." Xerxes isn't concerned with justice; he just wants to appear to be in control. He is doing impression management.

Xerxes' supreme court advises him to pass an edict that Vashti not be allowed to come before the king anymore (which probably doesn't break her heart since that is her crime in the first place) and that he get a new queen. As it says in verse 20, "Then when the king's edict is proclaimed throughout all his vast realm, all the women will respect their husbands, from the least to the greatest." Yeah, like that will happen!

Now, part of what's going on here is that the writer is showing us what flatterers these advisers are. They reinforce Xerxes' pride in his "vast and magnificent realm." They all know that the king's shadow mission is ego, appearance, and pleasure. "Make my kingdom about me" could be Xerxes' catchphrase. But these advisers don't name it, they won't challenge it, for the king has surrounded himself with people who will reinforce his shadow mission.

So Xerxes grabs on to their idea. He turns to his "personal attendants" for advice on the search. This is not the Supreme Court; these are his bodyguards, high-testosterone young men who give him their ideas of what to look for in a new queen. Want to guess their number-one criterion? They suggest he hold a "Miss Media and

Persia" beauty contest in which each province—127 in all—contributes one finalist to the royal harem. Then each contestant will go through rigorous beauty treatments, the ancient version of extreme makeovers. In the end, the young woman who best pleases the king will become the ultimate trophy wife.

It is hard for us, I know, to believe there was once a culture so superficial that middle-aged men would try to impress other people by showing they had so much wealth and power that they could attract a wife with youth and beauty. It is hard for us to believe that the human race ever descended to such depths, but once there was such a day.

Esther

One of the contestants is a young Jewish woman named Esther, adopted and raised by her cousin Mordecai. We're told she has a "lovely figure and [is] beautiful" (2:7). She makes it through the prelims and is one of the finalists selected to go before the king.

Think back to the last time you prepared for a big date. I mean when you really wanted to impress your date. How much time did you spend—on hair, face, wardrobe, fragrance? Ever spend just fifteen minutes? Ever spend an hour? Ever spend more time getting ready for the date than you actually spent on the date? Ever have more fun getting ready for the date than you had on the date?

Now look at Esther's date prep time. Not fifteen minutes, not a few hours, not even a day—but a whole year! Before a young woman's turn comes to go in to King Xerxes, she has to complete twelve months of beauty treatments: six months with oil of myrrh, and six months with perfumes and cosmetics (thankfully liposuction and silicone hadn't been invented yet). This is a lot of pressure for a first date. If someone isn't attracted to you after twelve months of prep time, it's probably not going to happen.

Esther, an elegant model of modesty and restraint, wins the contest and is named the new queen. The king throws another party.

BIBLE CHARACTERS WHO STOOD FIRM AGAINST THEIR SHADOW MISSION

Joseph stood firm against the temptations of revenge and sibling rivalry, choosing instead to forgive his brothers and to trust that God would redeem the evil he suffered.

. . .

Ruth refused to abandon her mother-in-law even though she could have pursued security and familiarity by returning home. She embraced loyalty and sacrifice over safety and became part of the adventure of redemption.

. . .

Daniel repeatedly refused to allow the lure of power to tempt him into compromising his convictions. From what he ate to how he prayed, he chose to honor God, even when it put his ambitions at risk.

. . .

Mary, the mother of Jesus. Her great response: "May your word to me be fulfilled" (Luke 1:38), meant she surrendered all dreams of a normal family life and (as an unwed pregnant woman) her respected reputation.

. . .

John the Baptist rejected the temptation of jealousy that his disciples voiced ("Look, [Jesus] is baptizing, and everyone is going to him,") by saying that his destiny and joy were to decrease so that Jesus might increase (John 3:26, 30).

It looks like Esther's mission is to be arm candy for the most powerful man on earth.

And Esther lives happily ever after, right? Not so much.

Haman

There's another character in this story. His name is Haman, and he is Xerxes' chief of staff. He is a much stronger leader than Xerxes is, but he too has a shadow mission. He is enraged because one man will not bow down and give him worship, and that one man is Mordecai—Esther's cousin and guardian.

Haman is so offended by Mordecai's gall in refusing to bow down to him that Haman goes to King Xerxes and offers him an enormous bribe. It's a huge sum, as much as the amount of money that all of the other countries controlled by Persia at that time would be sending in. All Haman wants is to be allowed to destroy Mordecai and Mordecai's people. And the king's response is basically, "Okay, whatever." He even tells Haman to keep the money. Xerxes doesn't really know which group Haman is ranting about. Because when leaders have been seduced by a shadow mission, they are not likely to challenge anyone else's shadow mission as long as it serves (or doesn't disturb) their own agenda.

Mordecai

When word of Haman's treachery reaches Mordecai, he realizes that there is only one person in the empire in a position to intervene with the king to seek to save all of Israel: the pageant winner. God's plan to save his people is placed in the slender hands of a beauty queen named Esther. And God reveals his mission for Esther through the words of a wise and trusted spiritual friend. "You must go to the king," Mordecai tells her.

Esther doesn't want to do this. She sends word back. Approaching the king unsummoned is a capital offense. And even if he deigns to hold out his gold scepter to her and receive her, he might not be so happy to hear her message that she doesn't like the way he's doing his job. The king is not real open to people defying him publicly. Esther knows what happened to Vashti.

And there is an additional glitch. Esther says, "The king has not summoned me for thirty days." She knows he has a full harem, and he is not a devoted husband. It is clear to Esther that the king is not as excited about her as he was in earlier days.

You have been brought to this point in your life not for yourself, but to be a part of God's plan to redeem the world.

At this point many people would back off. But not Mordecai. Mordecai challenges her. "Do not think that because you are in the king's house you alone of all the Jews will escape. For if you remain silent at this time, relief and deliverance for the Jews will arise from another place, but you and your father's family will perish." And he concludes his challenge with these magnificent words, "And who knows but that you have come to royal position for such a time as this?" (4:13–14).

With those few words, Mordecai names the beauty queen's true mission: *Esther, the fate of a whole nation, the fate of God's dream to redeem the world in human terms, at least as far as we can see it right now, rests in your hands. You have not been brought to this point in your life for the sake of accumulating an exquisite wardrobe and precious gems and exotic fragrances; you have not been brought to this point in your life to become the most desirable, attractive, applauded woman in the kingdom. You have not been brought to this point in your life for any of the reasons that the king thinks you have. You have been brought to this point to work for justice and to spare your people a great suffering. You have been brought to this point to oppose a man who is vile and evil and supremely powerful. You have a mission, Esther, and your mission matters. You have been brought to this point in your life not for yourself, but to be a*

BIBLE CHARACTERS WHO SUCCUMBED
TO THEIR SHADOW MISSION

Adam and Eve gave in to the original and still most popular shadow mission of all: "You shall be like God."

• • •

Solomon, who is supposed to the smartest guy in the world, ends up with a thousand-woman harem.

• • •

Judas refused to give Jesus access to that secret, bitter, selfish corner of his heart.

• • •

Herod could have been the champion and sponsor of the Messiah, but in his lust for power chose instead to be his rival.

• • •

Simon the Sorcerer had a shadow mission to have an impressive ministry. If you look closely, you may still find such shadow missions at work today (Acts 8).

---

part of God's plan to redeem the world. So, Esther, do not let your success at filling society's shadow mission for women blind you to what God says your mission really is. Esther, get a clue.

SHADOW MISSION REVEALED

To face a difficult truth without getting discouraged and defensive is one of the great challenges of a leader, and Esther manages to do just that. She tells Mordecai that she wants three days to withdraw with her closest friends for fasting and prayer. Being queen—which she thought was her greatest gift—has become her greatest burden. It is a call for sacrifice, maybe death. She's going to need strength beyond herself for this challenge.

Esther asks Mordecai to gather all of God's people in Susa for three days of fasting and prayer. She refuses to try to achieve this mission based on her beauty and her cleverness and her influence, though they are great. And with words that are as magnificent in their courage as Mordecai's were in their challenge, she declares: "When [the fast] is done, I will go to the king, even though it is against the law. And if I perish, I perish" (4:16). What a heart.

If you are a woman and God has gifted you to lead, for God's sake, for the church's sake, for the sake of this sorry, dark world, lead!

By the way, in a day when writers—even Christian writers—sometimes imply that women are relegated to the sidelines while the real action belongs to the men, it is ironic that one of the great heroes of the Bible is a woman who rejects the stereotype of the beauty queen, who subverts her dim-bulb husband, and who uses all her courage, initiative, and emotional intelligence to resist evil and work for good. So if you are a woman and God has gifted you to lead, for God's sake, for the church's sake, for the sake of this sorry, dark world, *lead!*

There were depths in Esther that even she did not suspect—as perhaps there are in you. A few years back there was a (possibly apocryphal) story that somebody at the doll factory messed up, and voice boxes intended for Barbie dolls ended up getting installed in G.I. Joes, and vice versa. Hundreds of kids were shocked to hear G.I. Joe say, "I hope I get asked to the prom!" And an equal number of young girls heard Barbie bark out, "Hit the ground now! Hard, hard, hard!" Xerxes thought he had married Barbie, but he ended up with G.I. Joe.

Impeccable Timing

On the third day, Esther puts on royal robes and stands in the inner court waiting for the king. Heart-pounding, nerve-racking suspense. Imagine what is going through her mind as she waits. *Life or death?*

The king sees Esther. He reaches out his scepter, the indication of royal favor. She will live for another day. He says, "What is it, Queen Esther? What is your request? Even up to half the kingdom, it will be given you" (5:3).

Esther understands this is the kind of thing a king says when he is in a good mood, but it isn't to be taken literally. If she had actually asked for half the kingdom, things would have changed radically. This was more or less king talk for, "Would you like to hold the remote control tonight?"

Esther couldn't blurt out, "I'd like to have you revoke the unalterable law of the Medes and Persians, spare my people, and put down your chief of staff." So she says, "I'm having a party. You and Haman come."

The king has never turned down a party in his life. So he goes to the party, and they have a great time. And the king says a second time, "Esther, what do you want? Even up to half the kingdom, it's yours."

And Esther says, "If the king regards me with favor and if it pleases the king to grant my petition and fulfill my request"—her verbal skills are remarkable—"let the king and Haman come tomorrow to the banquet I will prepare for them. Then I will answer the king's question" (5:8). Esther's negotiating skill here is phenomenal. The king, by agreeing to attend, has almost already agreed to her request. Her boldness, her intelligence, and her timing are breathtaking.

More...

We're ready now for the climax of the story, but the author leaves us in suspense for a moment. He switches back to Haman. Haman is very excited about what's going on. Haman is all puffed up in his spirit. He gathers together his wife and his friends, and he boasts about "his vast wealth, his many sons, and all the ways the king had honored him" (5:11). But then he complains, "All this gives me *no satisfaction* as long as I see that Jew Mordecai sitting at the king's gate" (5:13, italics added).

Haman has a shadow mission, and I mention this because many, many people in our culture face this one. It's maybe the greatest shadow mission of our society, and it's called "more." More wealth, more power, more applause, more status, more honors—*more*. And Haman goes through his life thinking, *If I can just get more, one day I will have enough.* But it never happens. The Rolling Stones may have recorded the song, but Haman sang it long before them, "I can't get no satisfaction."

Haman's wife advises him to have a gallows built seventy-five feet high and have Mordecai hung on it. Delighted by the suggestion, Haman has the gallows built.

That same night, King Xerxes can't sleep. He asks his servants to read to him (as king, he figures he doesn't have to read himself to sleep) from the annals of the king. "Read that book about *me*," he orders.

And they read to him the story of how a man named Mordecai once saved his life. When the king asks what recognition Mordecai received for his good deed, his servants reply that Mordecai has never been honored. At this moment, Haman arrives to ask the king to hang Mordecai, knowing nothing of the account just read to the king. And the king preempts Haman with a question: "What should be done for the man the king delights to honor?"

Sure that he must be that man, Haman tells the king that the man should be dressed in a royal robe and ride a royal horse led by a royal official and, for good measure, even the horse should wear a crown. "This is what is done," Haman says (nudge, nudge, wink, wink), "for the man the king delights to honor!" (6:9).

Imagine the moment. "Okay," says the king, "the man is Mordecai. Haman, you walk his horse through the city. You tell everybody he's the man I delight to honor."

From here on out it is all downhill for Haman. Esther holds another banquet and engages the king with courage and skill. She tells him that she and her people are to be destroyed.

"Where is he—the man who has dared to do such a thing?" asks the king.

"An adversary and enemy! This vile Haman!" the queen replies.

And Haman ends up being hung on the very gallows he had ordered built for Mordecai.

The king needs a new chief of staff, and Esther arranges that as well, appointing Mordecai over Haman's estate, which the king had given to her. Esther then returns to the king and reminds him that the edict that spelled death for her people is still in effect. The king gives her his ring and says, "Write another decree in the king's name in behalf of the Jews as seems best to you, and seal it with the king's signet ring—for no document written in the king's name and sealed with his ring can be revoked" (8:8). This new decree gives the Jews the right to defend themselves against Haman's terrorists. And the people of Israel become so feared, we're told, that "many people of other nationalities became Jews" (8:17).

Noble missions will give rise to noble thoughts, but shadow missions will produce an inner life of hidden darkness and destructive discontent. Shadow missions always destroy at least one person — the one who lives for them.

No Accident

This story tells us that our shadow missions have enormous destructive potential. The mission we devote ourselves to will shape us. Our unplanned, involuntary thoughts and wishes will spring out of it. Noble missions will give rise to noble thoughts, but shadow missions will produce an inner life of hidden darkness and destructive discontent. Shadow missions always destroy at least one person—the one who lives for them.

The story of Haman shows us another critical feature of shadow missions. They are almost always slight variations of our authentic missions. This is part of what makes them seductive. Rarely is somebody's shadow mission 180 degrees in the wrong direction. Our shadow missions generally involve the gifts and passions that have been hardwired into us. It's just that we are tempted to misuse them ever so slightly. Our shadow mission leads us just five or ten degrees off our true path in the direction of selfishness or comfort or arrogance. But those few degrees, over time, become the difference between light and shadow.

> *One thing is certain:* this *is your time. Now. Today. Not some other situation. Not tomorrow or yesterday.*

The story of Esther also suggests that perhaps where you are today is no accident. Who knows but that you have come to your position for such a time as this.

Esther did not set out to be queen, but once she was on the throne, she had to decide between a shadow mission of safety, wealth, and power versus her God-given mission of saving her people.

Haman could have used his position to promote justice, but gave in instead to his shadow mission of self-idolatry and cruelty.

The king could have embraced a mission of generosity, but instead settled for a shadow mission of shallow pleasure.

What is your position? Don't just think about your job or your leadership position. You also have influence through your family, your neighborhood, your volunteer commitments, and your friendships. One thing is certain: *this* is your time. Now. Today. Not some other situation. Not tomorrow or yesterday. We are often tempted to think that we are treading water right now, waiting for some other time, some more important position. You don't get to choose your time; your time chooses you. You are where and who you are for a reason.

JESUS' SHADOW MISSION

Did Jesus face a shadow mission? I think so. We are told by the writer of Hebrews that he, like us, was tempted "in every way" — but was without sin (4:15). For Jesus, the shadow mission was to be a leader without suffering, the Messiah without the cross.

The great New Testament scholar F. F. Bruce writes, "Time and again the temptation came to him from many directions to choose some less costly way of fulfilling that calling than the way of suffering and death, but he resisted it to the end and set his face steadfastly to accomplish the purpose for which he had come into the world" (*The Epistle to the Hebrews,* The New International Commentary on the New Testament, Eerdmans, 1990).

You remember that in the desert Satan tempts Jesus to achieve his mission without hunger, "Turn these stones to bread. You don't need to be hungry"; without pain, "Throw yourself down from the temple, and the angels will bear you up"; without opposition, "Bow down before me, and all the kingdoms of the earth will be yours." You don't have to be hungry, you don't have to hurt, you don't have to be opposed.

Later on, when Jesus tells the disciples he must suffer and die, Peter tries to convince him that his suffering is unnecessary. This is the same shadow mission, and that is why Jesus rebukes Peter so sharply, saying, "Get behind me, Satan!"

Jesus' shadow mission chased him all the way to the garden of Gethsemane. Again he wrestles with temptation, causing sweat like drops of blood to pour off him. "Oh, Father, let this cup pass from me. Not this."

Even when Jesus is hanging on the cross and people go past him and they're jeering him, what are they doing? It's the same temptation. "Look at him, he saved others, he can't save himself. Why don't you come down if you're the Messiah? There's no such thing as a Messiah that comes with a cross." But Jesus stares the shadow in the face, and at a cost we will never understand, not for all eternity, he says, "No, I will suffer. I will take all of the shadow of the dark, fallen human race on myself. I will go to the cross. I will drink the cup to its last drop." He does that for us. "Not my will, but thine be done."

Without Jesus' sacrifice, without the indwelling of his Spirit, none of us would have the self-knowledge, the courage, or the strength to battle our own shadow missions. We would be as self-absorbed as Xerxes, as unsatisfied and power hungry as Haman. We would be a mere shadow of the selves God intended us to be.

GIFTEDNESS AND CHARACTER

The battle between mission and shadow mission points to a fundamental distinction between two aspects of our makeup. There is a crucial difference between *giftedness* and *character.*

By *giftedness* I mean talents and strengths: high IQ, athletic ability, charm, business savvy, leadership skills, charisma, good looks, popularity, artistic talent. These gifts are very good things. They all come from God. The Bible says that he is the giver of "every good and perfect gift" (James 1:17), and that we should be grateful when such gifts come our way.

But your gifts are not the most important thing about you. There is something else you have that is called *character.* Character is your moral and spiritual makeup; it is your habitual tendencies, the way you think and feel and intend and choose. The makeup of what is called character is what makes people trustworthy or undependable, humble or arrogant. It's a word that sounds old-fashioned — kind of Victorian — but it is not. It is who we are at the absolute core of our personhood.

Character determines our capacity to be with God, to experience God, and to know God. It determines our ability to love and relate to other people. All that is part of our character. When we are called to imitate Jesus — to be "imitators of Jesus" — we are not being called to have his giftedness or his role. Rather, we are striving for his character.

Giftedness is good, but it's not the greatest good. It's important to be clear on this because we live in a culture that idolizes giftedness. This is the way, in our culture, that we get the "stuff" our culture tells us we ought to want. Giftedness is the path to the good stuff. Giftedness is what makes other people look at you and say, "Wow!" It puts people on magazine covers. Therefore, we are tempted to put more energy into wanting and enhancing our giftedness than paying attention to what is going on in our character and just slowing down and asking God to reform our character.

> *You can't envy good character. There's something about a Christlike character that is so good that even the desiring of it cannot harm us.*

When we idolize giftedness, we often end up envying other people's giftedness. I see someone else who is more gifted than I am in some area, and I wish that I had their gift, or I wish that they didn't have it. Their giftedness kind of sticks in my craw.

The desire for good character, however, never leads to envy. You can't envy good character. There's something about a Christlike character that is so good that even the desiring of it cannot harm us.

People who are highly gifted can use those gifts to pursue their mission or their shadow mission. People with well-formed characters recognize that their shadow mission is unworthy and undesirable.

In the absence of good character, the giftedness of people will not be used well. The more gifted we are, the more arrogant and self-centered and destructive we are apt to be. Lavish giftedness in the absence of well-formed character will always lead us toward our shadow mission.

SAMSON: CRUSHED BY GIFTEDNESS

There is a man in Scripture who is very gifted, but who doesn't have the character to bear his giftedness. Giftedness always comes at a price: pressures, temptations, a sense of entitlement. Without character, your giftedness will crush you. As it did Samson.

We read in the book of Judges, chapter 13, about how an angel of God comes to a childless couple and tells them they are going to have a son. He tells them God will gift their son lavishly, and the son must devote himself to God. He will be a powerful leader. He will deliver his people from living under the heel of the Philistines.

Their son, Samson, is to be a "Nazirite." This designation is an obscure idea taken from Numbers, the fourth book in the Old Testament, in which God says that if people want to devote themselves to him in a special way, they can enter into a season of commitment and devotion—a time when they take three vows to remind themselves of their commitment. First, they will touch no dead body. Second, they will drink no wine. And third, they will not cut their hair. There is nothing particularly virtuous about any of these promises. They are just temporary vows, but they are symbols, concrete reminders, that someone is devoted to do something for God. For Samson, these vows are to be a way of life. They are to help Samson cultivate a strong sense of his devotion to God. There will be certain options in his life that he needs to say no to, and vow-keeping will give him the inner strength to do so.

Samson grows up, a man of extraordinary gifts. He lives in a culture where physical strength matters, and he has it in spades. He can take a wild animal apart with his bare hands. He can defeat a dozen normal men in hand-to-hand combat. He is such a dazzling specimen that men want to be him, and women want to be with him. He has charisma, that kind of magnetism that makes people want to follow him into battle and adventure and into the unknown. He has power. He is what was called at that time in Israel a "judge."

Samson "da Man"

At that time, Israel did not have kings. Judges were the leaders of all the people. They were not like judges in our day where a person sits on a bench and tries cases. A judge in this time was the supreme political and military authority over all of Israel. Samson was the big dog, the alpha male. People would come up to him and say, "You da man, Samson." Samson would not say, "No, no, no. You da man." Samson would say, "You're right. I am da man."

I have tried to think of who he would be like in our day. He would be like a champion body builder with an incredible physique, but have the glamour of a movie star who could headline big-budget action flicks and maybe use that glamour to go into politics and become "Governator" of his entire state—that kind of a figure. Then add to all of that the fact that he had spiritual anointing. He was used by God.

One of the intriguing parts of his story is that sometimes God uses Samson *because of* what he does. And sometimes God uses Samson *in spite of* what he does. Samson's story shows us that even when there is spiritual anointing, even where there is impressive ministry, giftedness never makes up for a lack of character.

Samson, in quick succession, breaks two of the three Nazirite vows: he touches a dead body (the carcass of a lion he killed) in order to eat the honey inside. Because he never learned to say no to his appetite, he breaks his vow to God. Later, at a bachelor party he throws for himself, he drinks wine, breaking vow number two (Judges 14). But it's the breaking of the final vow that is the most famous—and most tragic.

The Has-Been Strong Guy

Samson falls in love with Delilah, a Philistine woman. Her being a Philistine is bad enough; the Philistines are about as far away from Israel's values and culture as they can be. They worship a god they call "Baal-Zebub" (2 Kings 1:2), Lord Baal. Their religion is so evil that cultic prostitution is an important part of worship of Lord Baal, as is infant sacrifice. This is so repulsive to the Hebrews that, as a term of derision, they call the Philistine god "Beelzebub." Does that sound familiar? *Beelzebub* is Hebrew for "Lord of the Flies." Beelzebub is a dark god associated with the place where flies gather—on a dung heap.

The Philistines begin to use Delilah to get to Samson—to find out the secret of his physical strength.

Delilah keeps asking Samson, "What's the secret to your strength?" He keeps making up answers. Finally she says to him, "How can you say, 'I love you,' when you won't confide in me? This is the third time you have made a fool of me and haven't told me the secret of your great strength" (Judges 16:15).

She continues to pester Samson until he is sick to death of it and tells her everything. This big,

> *If you don't develop the character to support your gifts, they will actually become destructive to you.*

strong man—this charismatic, magnetic leader—tells a nagging woman everything. "No razor has ever been used on my head," he says, "because I have been a Nazirite dedicated to God from my mother's womb. If my head were shaved, my strength would leave me, and I would become as weak as any other man" (Judges 16:17).

And now you understand the significance of the hair. This is the one vow Samson has never broken, and now, because he's hooked up with the wrong partner, because he never learned to say no to his appetites, because he never learned to tolerate frustration and disappointment, this man who was given such lavish gifts shreds the final vestige of his devotion to God and breaks the last vow. Now he is no longer a Nazirite; he's just a has-been strong guy.

You know the rest of this story. He goes to sleep. Delilah cuts off his hair and ties him up. When the Philistines come to take him away, Samson jumps up and thinks he will fight them. Then comes one of the saddest statements in the Bible: "But he did not know that the LORD had left him" (Judges 16:20).

He did not know.

Character is, among other things, the capacity to be inhabited by God. Every wrong choice, every dark thought I entertain, makes me a little less sensitive to the Divine presence. In the end, Samson's character was so eroded that he didn't sense its erosion or realize how absent God was from his life. The success of giftedness can mask the erosion of character. Samson did not have the character to bear his giftedness. In the end, the Philistines captured him and gouged out his eyes.

Ironically, it was not until Samson had lost his vision—not until he was blind, humiliated, and imprisoned—that he called out to God for help. But even in death his story is ambiguous. He asks for strength from God to "get revenge on the Philistines for my two eyes" (Judges 16:28). His life ends, as it was lived, in the ambiguity of the shadow: great power, a desire to serve God, mixed with a desire for vengeance.

CHARACTER FORMATION

Like Samson, you might be extraordinarily gifted. But if you don't develop the character to support your gifts, they will actually become destructive to you. Your shadow mission will win out and your gifts will crush you. It's only a matter of time.

You don't have a choice about what gifts you're given. But you *are* given a choice of what character you will build. Character—having the ability to grow in the character of Jesus—is available to anyone who wants it. But we don't live in a culture that exalts character. The challenge about Christlike character formation is that it's time-consuming, it's not very glamorous, and it won't get you very much at all ... except life with God ... except the healing of your broken, hungry, wounded, hurting, tired heart ... except the satisfaction of your soul ... things that giftedness can never achieve.

> *We can do really impressive-looking things, but what we take into eternity is* who we become.

To say it again: character formation is absolutely fundamental to our well-being, but it's not glamorous. So often—in our work, in our lives, even in our churches—we think, "Man, there's so much going on, we can't take the time to work on 'character.'" The question really is: Who do we want to be? We can do really impressive-looking things, but what we take into eternity is *who we become.*

So how do we go about doing this nebulous thing called "building character"? Well, character-building has one of those odd dynamics where you generally cannot pursue it directly. Somebody might say, "I'm gonna try really hard to be humble today." But trying really hard doesn't create humility. And if you manage to feel humble for a moment, your next thought is, *Wow, I'm being so humble, how come other people can't be more like this?*

When it comes to character formation, you need to use the principle of indirection. It's a bit like happiness. Joy, of course, is part of a healthy character, but you cannot pursue happiness by making it the primary focus of your life. Joy comes as a by-product of the pursuit of other things. And I believe that character comes as a by-product of the pursuit of God and the kingdom of God.

We cannot do character-building through moral self-improvement. The redeeming of our characters is a God-size job. But we are not passive. There are practices we can engage in that can help in character formation. Richard Foster wrote very wisely about this in his classic book *The Celebration of Discipline.* He identifies a number of practices that, when pursued wisely and with serious intent, can help lead to spiritual growth. So if, for instance, humility is something I really need to work on, I might engage in acts of service. Or if I use language to intimidate or exaggerate or deceive, then the practice of silence will be very important for me.

The idea of pursuing spiritual practices or disciplines can sound intimidating. In general, "discipline" is not a happy term in our day. But it's important to remember that these practices are all simply a means to an end. Anyone who is hungry for change in any area of life will pursue them. We think of ascetics back in the Middle Ages as being strange people. But many of the greatest ascetics of our day are playing in the NFL or performing in concert halls. They put their bodies through serious and wise training to be able to do what they deeply desire to do: sack quarterbacks or play "Stairway to Heaven."

Often in our day people think of training simply as something they do to develop their giftedness. But wise people have always understood that development of character also requires "training." We do this by asking what good character looks like. We ask, *What are the obstacles that keep me from having that kind of character? Am I prone to gossip, or laziness, or bitterness, or selfishness, or power, or apathy?* Then we ask, *What are the practices through which I might receive power to live a different kind of life?* Always, the goal of disciplines is freedom. I want to be free to do the right thing at the right time in the right way for the right reason.

> *We cannot do character-building through moral self-improvement. The redeeming of our characters is a God-size job. But we are not passive.*

One of the classic examples of shadow mission in our day is the problem of addiction. We have a friend named Sheila—tall, articulate, charismatic, bright—an Ivy League lawyer. But her shadow mission was to feel good. And eventually her shadow mission caused her to drink as much as possible as often as possible to avoid as much pain as possible. For a long time her giftedness got a lot of people to make a lot of excuses for her. But eventually she was told that one more bender would mean the loss of her job.

She bent. Again.

She ended up in the rehab ward of a psychiatric hospital. Her doctor told her to go to an AA meeting the first morning. She said, "I'm not going to go to a meeting with a bunch of drunks at 6:00 a.m." He replied, "Not only are you going, you're going to fix coffee for a bunch of drunks at 6:00 a.m."

She went. She fixed coffee. She joined the club. She began to follow the Twelve Steps. And through these practices—surrender, self-examination, confession, accountability, and so on—she began to receive the power to do what she could not do on her own. She received freedom from her shadow mission. One day at a time.

Find Your Mordecai

Character-building rarely happens in isolation. We'll never successfully battle our shadow mission if we don't have someone who will speak truth to us. Everyone needs a Mordecai.

What do I mean? Think back to the story of Esther. Do you think Esther would have given up her shadow mission of a life of ease and relaxing beauty regimens without the stirring challenge of Mordecai? Doubtful. Would she have realized the danger she was in? Doubtful. Would she have acted on it? Even more doubtful. Only from her trusted guardian Mordecai was she able to hear and accept a challenge, even when all her self-protective instincts told her to say no. Esther and Samson were perhaps the epitome of stereotypically gifted femininity and masculinity of their day. One of the biggest differences between them is that Esther had a Mordecai, and Samson did not.

Who is the Mordecai in your life? Who loves you enough to challenge you when you're ready to settle for your shadow mission? If you're part of an elder board or a leadership team, whether it's at your church or your workplace, do you have regular, honest, fearless conversations about the reality of your shadow mission? If you are in the leadership position on that team, do you model this, do you initiate it? If you are a leader and you do not know your shadow mission, I guarantee that you're the only one on your leadership team who does not know your shadow mission. Everybody else knows it, and they talk about it.

> *Who loves you enough to challenge you when you're ready to settle for your shadow mission?*

So find your Mordecai. A Mordecai is someone who is more devoted to the development of your character than impressed by your giftedness. Often this person is a spouse or close friend. But even those closest to you don't always see every aspect of your life. You'll need other family members or friends or colleagues who love you, people you can trust, people who can speak truth to you. Ask them to tell you when you're going down the wrong road. Then listen to them.

Name Your Shadow Mission

Up until now, I've been putting off the topic of identifying your shadow mission. First, I wanted you to understand the life-or-death consequences of shadow missions. And then I wanted you to be clear about how important character is in fighting your shadow mission, and how giftedness can sometimes blind us to the need for character. But now's the time to tackle it, because in order to fight your shadow mission you need to name your shadow mission. You can't fight the enemy if it doesn't have a name.

I've been through lots of exercises on developing a personal mission statement, and to tell you the truth, I've had a hard time coming up with a mission statement that sticks. I can identify the general areas about which I'm passionate, but coming up with a snappy, memorable, meaningful phrase—a catchphrase—has been difficult.

Not so with my shadow mission. I've known it since I was twelve years old, and I can sum it up in four words. I used to do some speaking when I was a little kid in our hometown. A newspaper reporter covered one of those occasions. The headline for the story was "Talkative boy wins acclaim." That's my shadow mission catchphrase. I know that, apart from God's help, my life would be an exercise in self-idolatry, a fruitless effort to win approval. I fight this shadow mission every day, and I will fight it the rest of my life. People I love get hurt by it.

I think of a man I talked to a while ago, a business leader in the corporate world. He was married with small children, and his family complained that he was never home. To this he said, "They don't understand; I'm doing it all for them."

"Really?" I challenged him. "Is it really true that you are doing it all for them? Why are you doing it for them when they don't want you to be doing it? If they did not exist, would your life look a lot different than it does now? Would you not be working the same way that you are?"

In reality, he was not doing it for them. It was clear who he was doing it for. In fact, his catchphrase could have been the exact opposite of what he'd said, namely: "They do understand; I'm doing it all for me!"

I think of a woman I know who was head of a faith-based educational organization. Smart as a whip. Tons of energy. Lots of drive. But her single most commonly used phrase was, "I'm sorry." Not "Let's take the hill." Not "We're lucky to be doing this." Not "Let's charge into tomorrow."

"I'm sorry."

And the dirty little secret, the truth behind all her apologies that no one knew—not even she knew—was that she wasn't sorry. She was afraid. And if you could have poked way down underneath the fear, I think you would have found some anger glowering around. I think she was mad at other people for not liking her when she was always so nice, and mad at herself for saying "sorry" so often when she wasn't.

For she had a shadow mission, though it was subtle. Her shadow mission was to be liked. Or to so out-nice everybody that if they didn't like her she could feel justified in judging them or dismissing their criticisms. Her shadow mission was so bathed in apologies that it almost looked radiant. But it was a shadow mission all the same. At the core it wasn't "nice" at all. It was all about avoiding conflict and evading unpleasantness and escaping criticism. It was, as all shadow missions are, truth-resistant. In the end, it sucked all the integrity and life out of her, and she left her calling. On her way out, in her farewell address to the troops, she said, "I'm sorry."

Just think of how much heartache could have been prevented if people were alerted to their shadow missions. That's why it's so important for you to seek out your shadow mission—so you can destroy it.

Before you try to name your shadow mission, however, it's a good idea to sit quietly for a while. Pray. Ask the Holy Spirit to open your eyes, for God promises to give wisdom to those who ask for it (James 1:5). Paul uses the image of a suit of armor because this kind of work is a battle—it requires the belt of truth, the breastplate of righteousness (character again!), the shield of faith (you can't do this on your own), the helmet of salvation (we don't even ride bikes without helmets anymore, and this is a lot more dangerous), and the sword of the Spirit (Ephesians 6:10–18; Hebrews 4:11–13).

Think back on the past. Ask: When have I failed? When have I felt shame? When has a gentle whisper indicated I've gone off track?

Read the list of "Top Ten Shadow Missions" (page 119). Recognize any of them from firsthand experience? Or did you see your own shadow mission reflected in the stories of Esther or Samson or some other Bible character?

Write down your reflections, if you're the writing type. Circle your temptations. Zero in on your failings. Then try to boil it all down to a sentence, then a catchphrase, maybe a single word. Run it past your "Mordecai" to see if someone who knows you well sees this in you.

A friend of mine went through this exercise. After some thought and prayer, here is how she summarized her shadow mission:

Sentence: I fall into living my shadow mission when I get so busy that accomplishing tasks becomes more important to me than loving God and my neighbor.

Catchphrase: To-do list all done.

One word: Busyness.

You may find that you battle multiple shadow missions. Their names are legion! For now, however, choose to focus on just one: the

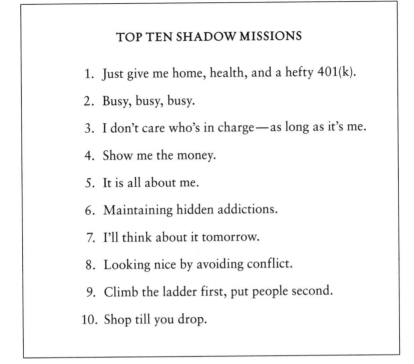

TOP TEN SHADOW MISSIONS

1. Just give me home, health, and a hefty 401(k).

2. Busy, busy, busy.

3. I don't care who's in charge—as long as it's me.

4. Show me the money.

5. It is all about me.

6. Maintaining hidden addictions.

7. I'll think about it tomorrow.

8. Looking nice by avoiding conflict.

9. Climb the ladder first, put people second.

10. Shop till you drop.

one you most want to hide. Work on that one for a while. There will be plenty of time to get around to number two. (Unless your number one is procrastination.) You really can trust that God will lead you in the process.

Finally, if, after all this, you still can't name your shadow mission, get outside help. Find your Mordecais and ask them!

Focus on Joy

Now that you've done all that heavy lifting in agonizing reflection and self-evaluation, it's time to take a break. Literally. One of the best ways to battle your shadow mission is by not focusing on it at all. Instead focus on joy. Non-strategic joy.

Strategic joy is the joy that comes from successfully executing a plan. As such, it often is tied in to a shadow mission.

Non-strategic joy has nothing to do with a person's success or ability or power. It just *is*.

Spending time with non-strategic people is a great source of pure joy. Wrestling with your kids on the floor. Mentoring that schoolchild in your community. Hanging out with your friends. Going on a date with your husband or wife. All of those things are incredibly helpful in providing non-strategic joy.

One of the best ways to battle your shadow mission is by not focusing on it at all. Instead focus on joy. Non-strategic joy.

For me, over the last year or so, a non-strategic source of joy has been golf. Now golf can be pretty close to a shadow mission in and of itself. I started playing it and I liked doing it. But golf doesn't help me achieve any goals or do anything important; to me it's just pure joy. And if I work out a little frustration by imagining someone's face on that tiny white ball as I hit it, all the better!

God gave us another amazing source of non-strategic joy: worship. Whether it's with a pipe organ or a praise team, with liturgy or laughing in the Spirit, pure unadulterated worship of God is the very best antidote to the shadow mission that darkens our hearts. Worship is (or should be) pure joy. Indulge in it regularly.

SHADOW MISSIONS IN ORGANIZATIONS

As my eyes have been opened to the idea of shadow missions, I've seen that they don't just afflict leaders. They also infect whole organizations.

The church I serve is just a couple of miles away from prestigious Stanford University in the heart of Silicon Valley. If Babel were built in the twenty-first century, this area probably would bid on the project. Venture capitalists and sleep-on-the-cot entrepreneurs and million-dollar fixer-upper houses and alpha techies live together in the land of billionaire dreams. Highly educated, highly affluent, highly overworked. The next community over is East Palo Alto, which, a few years ago, led the nation in murders per capita. But it is a world away.

The staff named the church's shadow mission years before I ever got there, just by nature of the location. They didn't use the phrase "shadow mission," but that's what they were describing. They sometimes joked that the motto of the church should be: "A successful church for successful people."

Just imagine if your church's shadow mission was posted on the sign out front or printed on its stationery. What might your telling catchphrase be? "We may not be growing, but we'll judge churches that are." "Successfully avoiding conflicts since 1893." "We take care of our own—and you're not one of us."

Businesses and nonprofits are not immune to acquired mission deficiency syndrome either. An accounting firm starts with a mission of giving honest feedback and financial practices to businesses—to help create accountability. But after a time the firm gets larger, draws more clients, and the mission shifts to "maintaining and increasing our bigness without getting caught at doing anything illegal." After a while, the "without getting caught" of that shadow mission decreases in importance. From that moment on the clock is ticking.

A corporation is born with a dream to provide energy for people that is inexpensive and good for the environment. Profits go up. Then the pressure becomes to increase the profits, even though it's at the expense of the original vision. The people at the top are described as giants by leading publications in their field. Eventually the mission becomes: "Maintain the vast egos of the people at the top." Mergers and kickbacks and dubious quarterly reporting strategies and lavish offices and bloated top-level financial practices all exist just out of public view; they are generally known inside the company. These strategies are indicators of the corporation's shadow mission.

An elected government official is so powerful that he engineers the downfall of numerous rivals, making it possible for him to virtually handpick the person against whom he will run. He keeps a list of his enemies. He encourages a culture in which those who report to him are ruthless in their arrogance and power. Eventually, whatever mission was present at the start is overtaken by the shadow mission, and the whole house of cards tumbles down.

A hi-tech corporation is so committed to opening up foreign markets that it allows its technology to be used by a totalitarian government to acquire information on political dissidents, who are then imprisoned unjustly. When this is made public, the hi-tech corporation's executives shrug their shoulders. Ethical scruples would be preferred, but must not be allowed to interfere with the shadow mission of global dominance.

A CEO hires detectives to spy on her staff and board because the shadow mission has become "Compliance and loyalty at all costs."

Heads of companies and real estate tycoons use books and seminars and TV shows to turn their faces and names into a brand, serving the shadow mission that declares: "Being the ultimate winner is everything."

LEADING YOUR TEAM INTO BATTLE

As the preceding examples reveal, identifying and battling your own shadow mission is good, but any good leader will also identify and battle the shadow mission of the company or church or organization that he or she leads. And the best way to do that is to alert the whole team to the concept of shadow missions, so that together you all know the face of the enemy you are battling.

Call a Retreat

If you lead a team, you may want to use some extended meetings or even a retreat to introduce and then probe the topic of shadow mission. It may be helpful for you to go off-site to give your team members distance from their day-to-day tasks so they can focus instead on these larger issues. And as with any retreat, be sure to include some fun to lighten up the mood and to encourage relationship building.

Depending on the existing team atmosphere and the relationships among your team members, this topic of shadow mission either has the potential to be intriguing and energizing or intimidating and threatening.

It helps for people to know that every human being and every organization wrestles with this. The question isn't *if* you have a shadow mission, it's if you'll deal with it. You may want to talk about the examples of some individuals or churches or companies or administrations that you have seen crippled by the shadow mission dynamic. Understanding what's at stake can help fuel people's energy for this discussion.

As a leader, you will be served by understanding a simple truth: Everybody who reports to you already understands your shadow mission—probably better than you do. A century ago a great scholar by the name of W. E. B. DuBois noted that African Americans had a great gift to give to white America—if white America would only accept it. It is the gift he called "double vision"—the ability to see the country from both the inside and the outside—because his people had been held outside by those with power inside. The shadow mission of those in power is seen most clearly by those who are under that power. So as a leader, if you're afraid to reveal the truth that you have a shadow mission to those who report to you, relax. They already know. They probably know your shadow mission better than you do.

When you sense that you and your team are ready to deal with this issue, begin your meeting, if you can, with a time of prayer. Give some thought to what the prayer will look like. You may want to spend some time in confession. Give people a chance to be honest before God about their own shadow sides. Then spend some time in prayer asking for grace. Take the time to receive forgiveness and mercy from God. Ask for illumination and wisdom. We are never able to see the whole truth about ourselves without God's help. Encourage people to ask God for wisdom about how to speak hard words with both truth and love.

The question isn't if you have a shadow mission, it's if you'll deal with it.

Then introduce the idea of shadow mission. Define it, explore it. You may want to hand out a copy of this book to each of your team members and have them spend time alone reading it and thinking about their own shadow mission. Discuss the general idea of shadow mission, but don't put anyone on the spot or ask anyone to name their own shadow mission unless they feel absolutely comfortable doing so.

You might think that publicly identifying one's own shadow mission may be more accepted or needed in a church setting than in a business setting, since in a church setting we are called to be spiritually accountable to each other. But I don't think this is the case. Patrick Lencioni, author of numerous bestsellers on leadership, writes that at the foundation of a healthy team is trust, and what is core to building trust is the appropriate vulnerability of a leader. True vulnerability can never be faked. It always comes with a little risk, a little pain.

Name Your Organization's Shadow Mission

Once you sense that everyone understands the concept of shadow mission, spend time as a team identifying or naming your organization's shadow mission. You might want to start by making a list of times when your team has gotten off track. That varies from team to team. For some teams it might be lack of structure or inability to take things seriously; for others it might be focusing on the wrong issues.

You might want to identify the indicators or warning lights that signal that a shadow operation is at work. Spend some time listing possible shadow missions in sentence form, catchphrase form, and as a single word.

How do you know when you've named your shadow mission? How do you know when you've put your finger on it? It's like the roar of a lion in the jungle; when you hear it, you *just know*. When it's named, there will be this little release of energy, maybe laughter, maybe embarrassment, certainly recognition. People on the team will say, "That's it! That's us!" One of the reasons we laugh at and remember catchphrases like "Successfully avoiding conflict since 1973" is that flash of recognition, an aha moment of "I'm like that" or "I know someone who's just like that." That's the moment you want to focus on with your discussion.

How do you know when you've named your shadow mission? How do you know when you've put your finger on it? It's like the roar of a lion in the jungle; when you hear it, you just know.

Finally, you may want to find a Mordecai—someone outside the organization who can address shadow mission issues with the whole team. Someone from the outside often can see things that people on the inside can't see. My wife is my greatest encourager and friend, and she is also my most effective Mordecai. I recently spoke at an event during the first week of January, and someone afterward said, a little hyperbolically, "That was the highlight of my year." My wife was standing next to me. Her immediate response was, "The year is young yet."

Form a Battle Strategy

Once you identify your team's shadow mission, spend time forming a battle strategy. List ways you can combat that shadow mission. Is there an accountability structure that needs to be formed? Is there a

---

TOP TEN SHADOW MISSIONS
FOR ORGANIZATIONS

1. Success for the sake of success.

2. A fearless squadron of yes-men.

3. Why risk walking on water when we can tread it?

4. People are made to be used.

5. Maintain the system.

6. Stay out of my silo.

7. It's all about politics.

8. Mastering the art of malicious compliance.

9. Cynicism R Us.

10. Avoiding accountability.

---

system or schedule or routine that needs to be changed? Is there a way you can keep that shadow mission in the forefront of the team's consciousness, a gentle or humorous way to remind your team of the shadow mission without becoming heavy-handed, negative, or annoying about it?

Probably the single most important tool in battling the shadow mission is solitude. Solitude is critical to the formation of human character. I find it striking that it was in solitude where Jesus came most excruciatingly face-to-face with his own shadow mission. It was during the forty days in the desert when the Evil One tempted him to be a messiah without hunger, without pain, without opposition. And it was in solitude that Jesus battled his shadow mission and was given the grace to say no.

As a leader, I need to regularly withdraw from the people and conversations and systems that normally surround me because even when they are filled with good intentions and constructive activities, over time I will be tempted to use them for the pursuit of my shadow mission. It is when I am alone that the shadow is unmasked. It is when I am alone that I remember no mission on earth can give me what I want most—which is to be loved and valued by my heavenly Father.

And what is true for me is true as well for the people who serve with me, who serve above me, who serve under me. We must withdraw from each other so that we are free of the need to impress or dominate or use each other. Then we are able to name our shadow missions to one another, to laugh about them, confess them, point out when they are reemerging, and call each other to a deeper mission.

It is also helpful to review our goals. What do we measure? If our shadow mission as an organization is "Be big," then we had better measure something other than just attendance. For instance, we could measure the number of times per year those of us in leadership serve food in a homeless shelter, or consistently volunteer our time in other ways.

Probably the single most important tool in battling the shadow mission is solitude. Solitude is critical to the formation of human character.

I'll give you another tool that may surprise you: read great literature. I know that to activist leaders, such reading can seem like a waste of time. But tragedies like *Macbeth* or *Hamlet* or *King Lear* are stories of shadow missions. Greek philosopher Aristotle said that one of the essential ingredients for an effective tragedy is that we must be able to identify with the central character. One of the purposes of tragedy is to knock us off our high horse, to help us humbly recognize our capacity for giving in to the shadow. However, as author Alain de Botton points out, the tone of modern culture and tabloid journalism often panders to the opposite emotion: how could those strange, pathetic celebrities/politicians/CEOs have such unthinkable flaws? He notes that if *Othello* were a modern-day story, the newspaper headlines would be something like "Love-Crazed Immigrant Kills Senator's Daughter." Or Oedipus, the king, might get "Royalty Caught in Incest Shocker" (*Status Anxiety*, Pantheon, 2004). The very act of leadership can reinforce our illusions of pride and omnicompetence. We read to understand that we all carry a Haman or a Samson or a Macbeth or an Othello inside our hearts.

> *One of the purposes of tragedy is to knock us off our high horse, to help us humbly recognize our capacity for giving in to the shadow.*

Restore the Strays Gently

Finally, as team leader, you need to be a sort of shepherd, looking out for team members who stray off track into their shadow missions, gently leading them back into the fold. Often when someone gets off track we tend to ignore the behavior, not wanting to make waves, or we tend to excuse it or rationalize it, especially if the person is a star performer. If we're removed from those who are straying, we may gossip about them or judge them. But none of those responses is helpful and, in the long run, they're positively harmful.

In Galatians 6:1, Paul says, "If someone is caught in a sin, you who live by the Spirit should restore that person gently." The operative word is *restore*. Restoration takes time; it takes wisdom; it takes thoughtfulness and gentle care. Even those in the business world have occasion to take disciplinary action. As Jesus pointed out, on those occasions the first step is to talk with the person face-to-face in private (Matthew 18:15).

Here's an example of someone doing that for me. About a month ago, I was talking with a close friend about a conversation I had with my wife, in which Nancy told me she felt I was being less than helpful around the house. I mentioned that my shadow mission at home tends to be self-preoccupation and passivity. And this friend said, "You know what, I see that in you. I have found myself lately thinking sometimes I want to talk with you or email you, but I hold back because I feel like I will be an interruption to you."

This friend didn't make any accusations. In fact, he wasn't charging me with anything. He was merely commenting on what he found going on inside of him as he related to me. He's somebody I'm quite close to, and it was painful to think that someone I care about could feel like he was an interruption. We had a long talk about it, and later I reflected on this quite a bit. I realized that when I go into shadow mission mode, I use my energy and giftedness to get people to applaud me, and the people close to me feel like I don't have time for them. It was a humbling realization.

When I go into shadow mission mode, I use my energy and giftedness to get people to applaud me, and the people close to me feel like I don't have time for them.

Whether you are battling an individual or a corporate shadow mission, some of the symptoms of the disease and strategies to fight it will be the same. For your convenience, I've summarized them in two sidebars (pages 130–132). Use these sidebars to jumpstart your own diagnosis and to form your battle strategy.

FROM SHADOW MISSION TO THE ONE VISION THAT MATTERS

While it's important to build your character and identify your shadow mission, in truth you need only one thing. Without this one thing you can name your shadow mission and claim it and battle

SYMPTOMS OF A SHADOW MISSION IN ACTION

A chronic sense of soul dissatisfaction. At work I feel less like a human being and more like a cog in a machine.

• • •

Emotional indicators. Irritability, lack of gratitude or joy, deep impatience, a sense of stagnation. Difficulty in achieving or maintaining motivation. When I slow down, I wonder: "Why am I doing this?"

• • •

A sense of smugness, exclusiveness, and self-congratulatory pride. I have a constant need to pump myself up by contrasting our organization with other organizations in our field that are less impressive.

• • •

Busyness at unimportant tasks. I have lost a sense of meaning in what I do. I default to rote compliance rather than genuine engagement.

• • •

Relationships are superficial. People become objects to use. Anonymity is pervasive. People do not know each other outside the cubicle. Supervisors do not care about the lives and families and interests of those they supervise. Few friendships happen at work. People feel unknown.

• • •

Self-aggrandizement. My gifts are used not to glorify God, but to gratify myself.

• • •

Lack of authenticity. Leaders give motivational speeches, but the tone feels hyped up, contrived, manipulative. Missing are simple, sincere descriptions of why what we do matters. People give surface responses, but underneath is widespread complaining and withdrawal, expressed covertly and destructively.

. . .

Running on empty. There is a sense among the staff that the organization is spending down the relational reserves that were built up in earlier, healthier, more devoted days.

. . .

Loss of excellence. It is no longer clear to people what it looks like to be effective. What was once a clear and compelling vision is increasingly replaced by "complaint management" or "survival" behaviors.

it—and still lose. That one essential thing is a vision of God and the reality of his kingdom.

The Reformation. The Great Awakening. The Jesus People Movement. As Dallas Willard points out in his fabulous little booklet *Living in the Vision of God*, any great movement of God begins with a vision. That vision is not about what the person or church or movement is going to do. It's not even a vision about the future.

The vision that really matters is the vision of how good God is and how blessed I am to be his child. This vision, of an already existing reality, sees the goodness and competence of God. Then out of the goodness of that vision grows a desire to do something for God, to make his kingdom real. Because God's work is all-comprehensive,

STRATEGIES FOR BATTLING
YOUR SHADOW MISSION

Spend time in solitude and silence. Make time for solitude—for yourself and for other members of the team—so you can come to clarity about what your shadow mission is.

. . .

Be humbly open to truth. Read great literature with a repentant spirit.

. . .

Be honest. Name your shadow mission with courage, precision, and humor.

. . .

Identify the consequences. Reflect together how destructive it would be to give in to the organization's shadow mission and recommit to fight it.

. . .

Quantify progress. Decide how to measure and clearly gauge movement away from the shadow mission.

. . .

Celebrate. As a team, regularly celebrate progress in moving toward your organization's true mission.

the need for this vision is as great for business or for schools as it is for local churches. All human work is meant to be rooted in what God is doing.

Over time, as a movement or organization or church grows, people start to focus on what's growing rather than on the reality of God. And then the shadow mission replaces the kingdom of God vision. Once that happens, it's just a matter of time before everything falls apart. Questions like these get in the way: How do we make this thing bigger? How do we make it better? How do we at least keep it propped up? And we become preoccupied with numbers, goals, and programs, and people live with stress, exhaustion, fatigue, and competition. Before we know it, we've not only lost the essential God vision but we've lost our true mission and slid into shadow mission.

The only safe way to lead a team is to be rooted in this God vision. It's not a vision of what might happen someday. It's a vision of what already *is*. It's a vision of God and the goodness of God. If I can live in that vision, then I will seek to do good things with God, and I won't be clutching onto outcomes in a life-or-death manner.

When I first arrived at the church I serve, I realized what a mistake it is to begin: "Okay, here's where we're going. Here's where I'm going to lead you." Instead, we had to learn together to start with the reality of God. With what a good God we worship. With living in the freedom and joy of God's presence.

I also realized I could not lead people I did not know and who did not know me. My temptation can be to think leadership means casting a spellbinding vision and having people ask how high they should jump.

Over time, as a movement or organization or church grows, people start to focus on what's growing rather than on the reality of God. And then the shadow mission replaces the kingdom of God vision.

But that's not the way it goes. Because in the trenches and in the pews, people are wondering, *Who is this person and why does he or she want to do this?* The need for relationship and trust is basic.

> *Once a group is focused on the goodness of God and on living in meaningful relationship with each other, they can do great things.*

But once a group is focused on the goodness of God and on living in meaningful relationship with each other, they can do great things. People's lives are changed. The hungry are fed. The poor are cared for. The business and its workers thrive. And a little bit of God's kingdom gets planted and grows here on earth.

THE BENEFITS OF STAYING ON MISSION

We've looked at the negative consequences of succumbing to a shadow mission. There's dissatisfaction, restlessness, boredom. At its worst there's scandal or even death. But what does life look like if we successfully battle our shadow missions? What might our teams achieve if we are able to stay on mission? Is life suddenly rosy?

The surprising answer is: not necessarily. Your life may actually get harder. Not in a destructive way, not in a negative way. But you might discover there's a lot of work to be done. You might need to deal with a certain person. You might have to raise some capital. You might have to make a change that people will criticize. Living on mission doesn't mean your life will be more fun or easier.

But it does mean your attitude will change. Instead of covertly focusing on yourself and the needs of your own ego, you are free to care about your organization. You are able to long for the flourishing of your group, even apart from yourself. I've noticed that when everything is about me—my need to achieve, my need to have success, my need even to survive—the team stumbles. But when I'm able to give up even the need for a good outcome, I can live in freedom.

I'll tell you a story that illustrates this principle of living in freedom. A couple years ago we invited Dallas Willard to speak at our church. After he finished his talk, I walked him out to his car. He had to go to another venue. As we walked, he was just kind of shuffling along, humming this hymn, this goofy hymn ... not even humming it well.

What struck me was that usually when people finish giving a talk, their next thoughts are, *How'd it go? How did I do? Did I do okay? Did people think it went well?* And if they think it went well, they feel good. Or if they think it went badly, then they start to feel kind of bad. As a speaker, I wrestle with that, and I see it in most folks who speak in public. But with Dallas, it was like watching a kid let go of a helium balloon. The balloon goes up like this ... and it's gone ... it's just gone.

I had heard Dallas talk before about the necessity of letting go of outcomes. As leaders, we need to be aware of outcomes, we need to take them seriously and learn from outcomes, but we should not carry the burden of them. Outcomes are in God's hands. We were not meant to carry them. We must not allow outcomes to crush us. But hearing Dallas talk about letting go of outcomes is one thing. To watch him give a talk and then just let it go ... it was remarkable.

I'd love to have that kind of freedom. But there would be a loss in having it. Because I would have to let go of the narcotic of living off of the applause when something goes well. And I would have to humble myself to realize that I'm part of something far greater than myself.

> *I've noticed that when everything is about me — my need to achieve, my need to have success, my need even to survive — the team stumbles.*

GOD'S GREAT MISSION

Here is the great news: our little missions are part of a *much bigger* mission. They are part of God's great mission that has been sealed by something far more powerful than our gifts or even our character.

Just look at what was going on behind the scenes in the book of Esther. Esther, as you may know, is the only book in the Old

Testament that never mentions God, but in reality he's the main character in the story.

There is a law that's unalterable in this story. There is a will that will not be turned, but it ain't the law of the Medes or the Persians. How is it that, of all the women in the empire, a young Jewish woman named Esther becomes queen? How is it that, of all the people in the empire, Mordecai should be the one who saves the king from an assassination plot? How is it that the king should have insomnia on the very night that Haman builds a gallows for Mordecai—that of all the stories, the one read to the king was the one of Mordecai saving his life? How is it that Haman, the scheming murderer, becomes the victim of his own schemes, and Mordecai, his intended victim, becomes instead his replacement? How is it that the king's ring, given to Haman, ends up on Mordecai's finger? How did the noose intended for Mordecai end up around Haman's neck? How is it that the people who marked the Jews for destruction are themselves destroyed?

The writer wants us to know that even in exile, as God's people were then—with no Jerusalem, no temple, no Sanhedrin—God is present. Unseen, unnamed, he is at work behind the scenes, and his purpose is certain.

You can die to your shadow mission and lead with joyful freedom because God is always at work in and around you in unseen, unknown, unnamed, and unlikely ways. He's in a manger, in a desert, on a cross. He's at work behind the scenes in wars and famines and floods and disasters. He is present in both dictatorships and democracies. And he's got his hand on churches, businesses, organizations, and individuals everywhere. God wants to use you *because of* what you do (your mission), but—as Samson shows us—he will also use you *in spite of*

Here is the great news: our little missions are part of a much bigger mission.

what you do. He can turn even your shadow mission into something he can use to his glory and the coming of his kingdom here on earth.

Does this mean we can indulge our shadow mission with impunity? Of course not. As Paul wrote, "What shall we say, then? Shall we go on sinning so that grace may increase? By no means! We are those who have died to sin; how can we live in it any longer?" (Romans 6:1–2) Instead, Paul instructs us, "Offer yourselves to God ... as an instrument of righteousness" (Romans 6:13). At one time we might have been slaves to our shadow missions, our shameful desires for fame, fortune, power, pleasure, or security. But now we can become servants of God, increasingly desiring his kind of life and active in his mission for the world.

Not a shadow mission. Just a simple, daily, humble, stretching, joyful peace that you and I can call each other to in the work of him who is light, in whom there is no darkness.

Who knows but that you have come to your position for such a time as this.

Just Walk Across the Room Curriculum Kit

Simple Steps Pointing People to Faith

Bill Hybels with Ashley Wiersma

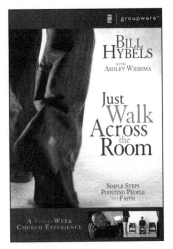

In *Just Walk Across the Room*, Bill Hybels brings personal evangelism into the twenty-first century with a natural and empowering approach modeled after Jesus himself. When Christ "walked" clear across the cosmos more than 2,000 years ago, he had no forced formulas and no memorized script; rather, he came armed only with an offer of redemption for people like us, many of whom were neck-deep in pain of their own making.

This dynamic four-week experience is designed to equip and inspire your entire church to participate in that same pattern of grace-giving by taking simple walks across rooms—leaving your circles of comfort and extending hands of care, compassion, and inclusiveness to people who might need a touch of God's love today.

Expanding on the principles set forth in Hybels' book of the same name, *Just Walk Across the Room* consists of three integrated components:

Sermons, an implementation guide, and church promotional materials provided on CD-ROM to address the church as a whole

Small group DVD and a participant's guide to enable people to work through the material in small, connected circles of community

The book *Just Walk Across the Room* to allow participants to think through the concepts individually.

The Power of a Whisper

Hearing God, Having the Guts to Respond

Bill Hybels

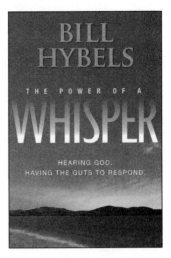

"Without a hint of exaggeration," says Bill Hybels, "the ability to discern divine direction has saved me from a life of sure boredom and self-destruction. God's well-timed words have redirected my path, rescued me from temptation and re-energized me during some of my deepest moments of despair."

In *The Power of a Whisper*, vision is cast for what life can look like when God's followers choose to hear from heaven as they navigate life on earth. Whispers that arbitrate key decisions, nudges that rescue from dark nights of the soul, promptings that spur on growth, urgings that come by way of another person, inspiration that opens once-glazed-over eyes to the terrible plight people face in this world—through firsthand accounts spanning fifty-seven years of life, more than thirty of which have been spent in the trenches of ministry, Hybels promotes passion in Christ-followers' hearts for being wide open to hearing from God, and for getting gutsier about doing exactly what he says to do. For more information go to: www.thewhisperwall.com.

Available in stores and online!

THE GLOBAL LEADERSHIP SUMMIT

The Summit is live from the campus of Willow Creek Community Church near Chicago, IL, and reaches more than 185 host sites across the United States. In the months following, the Summit moves into more than 200 cities in 70+ countries across the globe.

Best experienced with the entire leadership core of your church or organization, the Summit unifies teams through shared experiences, common vocabulary, and high-level teaching and inspiration.

It's more than a two-day event. Increasingly, the Summit is a leadership movement that has united hundreds of thousands of leaders across the globe—people like you, seeking to maximize the impact of their churches or organizations and bring the hope of Christ to our broken world.

Attend the Summit and join this leadership movement.

willowcreek.com/summit

Share Your Thoughts

With the Author: Your comments will be forwarded to the author when you send them to *zauthor@zondervan.com*.

With Zondervan: Submit your review of this book by writing to *zreview@zondervan.com*.

Free Online Resources at
www.zondervan.com

Zondervan AuthorTracker: Be notified whenever your favorite authors publish new books, go on tour, or post an update about what's happening in their lives at www.zondervan.com/authortracker.

Daily Bible Verses and Devotions: Enrich your life with daily Bible verses or devotions that help you start every morning focused on God. Visit www.zondervan.com/newsletters.

Free Email Publications: Sign up for newsletters on Christian living, academic resources, church ministry, fiction, children's resources, and more. Visit www.zondervan.com/newsletters.

Zondervan Bible Search: Find and compare Bible passages in a variety of translations at www.zondervanbiblesearch.com.

Other Benefits: Register to receive online benefits like coupons and special offers, or to participate in research.

ZONDERVAN®

ZONDERVAN.com/
AUTHORTRACKER
follow your favorite authors